THE PARSIS

OR

MODERN ZERDUSTHIANS.

THE PARSIS;

OR

MODERN ZERDUSTHIANS.

A SKETCH

BY

HENRY GEORGE BRIGGS.
Author of The Cities of Gujarashtra

ISBN: 978-93-5128-467-3(HB)

First Published in 1852
Indian Reprint in 2017

Published by

Kalpaz Publications
C-30, Satyawati Nagar,
Delhi – 110052
E-mail: kalpaz@hotmail.com
Website: kalpazpublications.com
Ph.: +91-9212142040

DEDICATED TO

ARTHUR ST JOHN RICHARDSON, ESQ.,

(OF THE BOMBAY CIVIL SERVICE,)

ORIENTAL TRANSLATOR TO THE GOVERNMENT OF BOMBAY,

IN TOKEN OF

RESPECT AND GRATITUDE.

PREFACE.

Adopting a popular custom, this Preface has been written.

Centuries ago, the knight who girt on his panoply of steel had to assign a reason for so doing; such, it appears, must also be the case for assuming the *steel-pen of modern authorship.*

I had been asked to furnish some information in a collated form regarding the Pársís, as all that could be obtained was mixed up with theological discussion in Dr Wilson's valuable works. In endeavouring to meet the wishes of the party, I found my manuscripts swell so alarmingly that I determined upon having recourse to the Press. This purpose is now accomplished.

I have had a delicate and trying duty before me, with the mass of materials and the variety of sources of information at my control. Not one line of this publication has been penned, however, with any unkind feeling; and I would indeed be pained to know that I had unconsciously given offence.

As pertinent to the subject I might have dedicated this volume to one of the Pársí community,—to the venerable Sir Jemshedjí Jíjíbhái,—or to the worthy Shet Káuvasjí Jehángír, (and "none worthier than he,")—or to the highly respected Shet Frámjí Nasarvánjí,—but that I had determined not to lose the opportunity to notice a name that to me must ever be associated with obligations.

I have endeavoured to be both easy and agreeable in the style; and have avoided references in detail to works, few of which may be found here, and many of which are not even known by name to the generality of readers.

CONTENTS.

SECTION IV.

SECTION V.

APPENDIX.

KEY TO THE READING OF NATIVE NAMES.

---

a as in *donatist.*
á — *part.*
e — *rest.*
í — *filial.*
u — *rueful.*

THE PÁRSÍS;

OR,

MODERN ZERDUSTHIANS.

SECTION I.

Nature of Information already before the European Public —Object of present Publication—Battle of Náhávand, and Defeat of the Natives of Irán—Their Wanderings, and Landing in India—Early European Travellers who have said anything of them—Their present Numbers, and how dispersed.

The spiritual philosophy of the early occupants of Irán, and the peculiar characteristics of that philosophy and of its founder, have not unsuccessfully engaged the attention of the learned. The dynasties that succeeded the glorious enterprise of

Káiomarz,—their laws, their institutions, and the economy of their rule,—their manners, their pastimes, and their domestic arrangements,—the strength of their army, their instruments of offence and defence, their mode of warfare, and their various achievements,—have been already so clearly and so ably described as to defeat repetition, unless it partake of plagiarism. The labours of Schlegel, Anquetil du Perron, the Abbé Foucher, Rask, Stuhr, Bopp, Purgstall, Westergaard, Burnouf, and other eminent men on the continent of Europe, and, among our own countrymen, Hyde, Dean Prideaux, Gibbon, and Sir William Jones, Forbes, Erskine, and Romer, all three of the Bombay Civil Service; Dr Drummond, the author of the first work on the Gujarátí dialect; Major Price, General Vans Kennedy, and Dr Wilson, have done much to clear many hitherto dubious points. Both Sir John Malcolm and Sir Gore Ouseley, in their political embassies, endeavoured to obtain much valuable information, and have elucidated several interesting data in their respective works on Persia. Not a little, too, has been done by Mr Bailie Fraser, and other travellers in Persia, and the publications of those who have visited the banks of the Tigris and the Euphrates, and have seen the ruins of the city of the Khálífs, have all contributed important facts, even when considered by them of a trivial character, so long as they were incidental. A humbler task offers itself to the writer.

Observations have been occasionally hazarded regarding individual members of the community of Zerdusht, or regarding such of their peculiar traits as were significant to tourists—instance, Colonel Fitzclarence,* Captain Basil Hall, Miss Emma Roberts, Mrs Postans, and a number of contributors to the public press; but the desultory nature of these observations has prevented that notice being paid to the community, as a distinct community, that it

* Afterwards Earl of Munster.

deserved. The present sketch of the Pársís of our day, and of the generation previous, from information derived from members of the tribe both in Gujarát and in Bombay, will, it is hoped, serve to fill this gap.

For those who have not given the early history of the Pársís even the most passing attention, the writer will briefly run over a few facts which may prove interesting, as well as of service, in the perusal of the matter to follow. With the dawn of the seventh century the Arabs commenced their inroads into Persia, and in the reign of Yezdíjírd, the last of the Sassanian dynasty, circumstances favoured the accomplishment of their intentions. At the battle of Kádseáh, the
A. D. 638. Persian army, under Rustam
A. H. 17. Ferokhzád, was almost wholly decimated, with the loss of the apron of Káwá, the celebrated Daraphsh-e-Káwání, the Imperial Standard which victories, renown, and confidence, had enlarged and decorated with costly gems. Nearly three years afterwards, upon the recall of Sáad

ben Wákás, the General of the forces of the Khálífet, Yezdíjírd collected an army of 150,000 men, and, under Phíráuzín, an officer of tried valour, hazarded the fortunes of his house and his people. Impelled by the religious fanaticism of their race, the Arabian army was largely recruited, and the combatants seemed equally intent to venture upon some decisive purpose. The army of the Arabs was commanded by Nomán ben Makrán Mazanní, and under the orders of the Khálíf Omár. The conflicting hosts met at the site of the Persian encampment. An obscure hamlet, called Náhávand, situated forty-five miles to the south of Hamadan, the ancient Ecbatana, and the site of a cenotaph to the memory of that Artaxerxes, the Ahasuerus of Biblical writ, and his beautiful wife the Hebrew Esther, became at once the scene of the last glorious purposes and the annihilation of that monarchy consolidated by Khái Khasru, the Cyrus of the Greeks, whose dying words have been so elegantly Anglicised in rhyme

by our Denham. For two months the respective forces kept aloof, except in partial sallies, or indifferent skirmishes; for two months they lay before each other, without effecting any important purpose, when the impatient spirit of Nomán drew up his forces in battle array, sounded the pious war-cry of "Allá Akbár!" and charged the Persian host with irresistible fury. The consequences were too fatal. The carnage of Náhávand passed the empire, from the followers of Zerdusht to those of Muhammad. The wretched Yezdíjírd led a precarious life, chiefly spent in wanderings, for the next ten years, when he was murdered by a
A. D. 641. miller eight miles from Merv.
A. H. 21. His General, Phírauzín, was killed by a body of horsemen from the field of Náhávand, who pursued the warrior into the hills where he had taken flight. Such as would not embrace the faith of the conquerors either fled to the wild fastnesses of the Khurásán mountains, or betook themselves to the still more desolate plains of their

father-land. About half a century afterwards a considerable number sought safety in flight from the persecutions of the new lords of their country. With this purpose they proceeded first to the island of Hormazd, or Ormus, in the Persian Gulf; after a stay of fifteen years they made way to Dívá or Diu, at the South-eastern extremity of the Katiwád peninsula. Here the fugitives are said to have remained some nineteen years, and from thence to have gone on to Sanján, in Gujarát, where they debarked about A. D. 717. At Sanján they settled for three hundred years, and from there spread troops of enterprising young men in the populous cities adjacent. History is then silent of their proceedings, until the beginning of the sixteenth century, when they afforded their support to the Hindu monarch of the territory in which they dwelt against the aggressions of Sultan Mahmud Begada. The occasion rendered them careful of their sacred fire, which was conveyed into the Wásandá jungles, and upon the retreat of the Muslim sovereign of Ahmedábád, this venerated property was removed to Náusárí, at the expense of two opulent members of the tribe.

With the presence of Europeans in the country the peculiarities of the Pársís gained them no ordinary notice, and the vestige of a people almost lost to the world won the credulity and exercised the ingenuity of every marvel-seeking gossip in Christendom, and lent the traveller greater importance than the assertions of his narrative. Osorio, Faria e Souza, Pietro de la Valle, Olearius, in his edition of the posthumous papers of Mandleslo,—Sir Thomas Herbert, Sir John Chardin, Thevenot, Kœmpfer,—all make mention of them. Hamilton, the mariner, tells an excellent story of a Pársí, who took him over the scene of a contest between the Portuguese and our countrymen, and who showed the skulls of those that fell on the occasion. Sir Nicholas Waite, one of the early Governors of Bombay, had a Pársí as his broker, who appears to have been the quintessence of mischief. Ives furnishes a sketch of a *Dokma*, or Tower of Silence. Henry Lord, the first Chaplain to the Surat Factory, published an account of the Pársís and their faith in 1630. The Rev. Mr Ovington, another Chaplain in the East India Company's service, also said a good deal about the Pársís some fifty years subsequently. Dr Fryer, Carsten Niebuhr—the great Arabian traveller, Careri—an Italian Doctor of Civil Law, and many others whose names are not so familiar to the world of literature, also contributed their quota of information. Independent of historians, antiquaries, and travellers, translators of the works of the Pársís, like Eastwick, Atkinson, and several who have versified their chronicles, the poets of Europe, too, have drawn upon them for imagery and delightful illustration, particularly the idea of the adoration of Sol. Moore has afforded the Fire Worshipper a conspicuous position in his "Lalla Rookh," and in that gorgeous tale of chivalry, "Ivanhoe,"

Sir Walter Scott bestows a hymn to Ahriman.

Of the present numerical strength of the Pársís, there are about 5000 at Yazd and Kirman, in Persia, according to M. Westergaard, of Copenhagen, who visited their settlements in 1843 under a scientific mission from his monarch, the King of Denmark. From the Census of the island of Bombay on the 1st May 1849, the following returns are given:—

	Males.	Females.
Under 14 years of age ..	13,496	13,437
From 14 to 50 years ..	39,192	32,325
From 50 to 80 years ..	8,279	7,969
	60,967	53,731

Or in all 114,698 souls: an average proportion of females to males as 88 to 100, or a relative proportion of females to males under 14 years, as 99 to 100; under 51 years, 82 to 100; under 81, 90 to 100; or, in their comparative ratio to the maximum or aggregate, of youth 23·4 per cent., adults 62·3, and the aged 14·1. The community at

Surat muster strong, though not in such numbers as half a century ago: to include all those in the various towns of Gujarát, as Broach, Baroda, Khambaiyat, Ahmedábád, and Damán, and at their religious strongholds, as Nausárí, Gandeví, Udíwádá, and Balsár, with the few families scattered about the Northern Konkan, there are about 20,000 adults. Of all the tribes now indigenous to the soil of British Hindusthán, the Pársí must command our warmest and most lively sympathy. He has proved the best suttler to our forces through Sindh, Beluchisthán, the country of the Afgháns, the Cis-Sutlej, and the newly-absorbed empire of Lahor. He is generally the mess-agent at the different military stations of the Bombay Army, and is also to be seen in particular localities of the Bengal and Madras Presidencies. Impelled by the same spirit of commercial adventure, he is to be met in the several British Consular Ports of China, but principally at Canton; in some numbers also at Macao and Hong-Kong, at Singapore,

Penang, Batavia, Rhio, Ceylon, and Aden. Stray individuals have also settled in New South Wales, Mauritius, and the Cape of Good Hope; a few are at Madras and on the Malabar Coast, and the number of those at Calcutta has largely increased of late years.

SECTION II.

Personal Appearance — Disposition — Costume — Education and Employment of Men and Women — Publications — Mode of Living — Occupations — Diseases — Morals and Crime.

THE physiognomy of the Pársí partakes of the general type of features peculiar to the western peninsula of Asia, as seen in the Arab, the Persian, the Armenian, and in those tribes and diversities of people dwelling in the plains or highlands to the east of the Mediterranean Sea. If one class more than another approximate to positive resemblance it is the Armenian,—there is the same bold formation of countenance, the fine aquiline nose with the well-developed nostrils, large black eyes, a well-turned chin, the unusual length of ears, the sensual character of the lips, and the heavy eyebrows. Pársís are taller, larger, and heavier in physical formation, and more athletic than the indigenous natives of Híndusthán. Their women, when young, are really handsome; but after the age of sixteen they become gross in appearance, and a few years make them corpulent and waddling in their gait. The women bind a luxuriant head of hair with a handkerchief, denominated the *pewan;* the men shave the head like all Orientals, but wear a moustache universally, whereas but a few adopt whiskers, and the *Mubeds*, or priesthood, only cultivate beards, and permit the hair of the head to be unshaven. Many of the Pársís are as fair in complexion as Europeans, without any of that ruddy tint peculiar to the children of the north; the preponderating hue is that sallow which long residents in Híndusthán, even Europeans, eventually wear. That the emigrators from Irán possessed a fine colour not a doubt can be held—instance the descendants of Arabian Jews, who have resided for centuries in India. Upon the same principle it may fairly be contended that the numberless dark or olive-hued Pársís arise from early intermarriages or concubinal intercourse with the natives of this country.

In disposition the Pársí is inclined to be sprightly—nay, even jocose; he is benevolent; affords encouragement to mendicity from the same charitable impulse rather than to purchase any merit; fond of entertaining his friends, however indigent in means, or humble in position; a *gourmand* in point of living, and an undoubted *bon vivant;* alive to every amusement, and keenly sensitive to the promotion of every sensual enjoyment.

The costume of the Pársí is also peculiar to himself. The *kustí*, or sacred cord, which passes round his body, is enjoined by his creed, and his *sadrá*, or shirt, is also a matter arranged by spiritual dictum. The other portions of his dress are most certainly of Gujarátí origin. His *angrakhá* is a long cotton coat, extending to the knees, closely tied in a bow at the throat and at the waist; the arms of the coat are, however, almost twice in length those of his natural possession, simply to permit their being closely and prettily drawn in puckers. The *pyjámá* (loose drawers, supported at the waist by a cord drawn through an open hem) is of silk, with those who can afford to purchase such material, and of cotton with the poorer classes. The *pagrí*, or turban, generally of a dark chocolate or maroon colour, sprinkled with sprigs, or other like small fanciful design, is composed of several yards of cloth arranged upon a mould, in consequence called *gábho*. It is always worn abroad, and even within doors, except at meals, when the skull-cap, used under the turban, is allowed to remain on the head. It would be disrespectful to uncover the head in the presence of a superior, or even a friend; but this prejudice appears to be wearing away. The Chinese have contrived to form a lighter weight for the head, by starching single folds of the outer materials, with a kid-leather lining within, something after the fashion of the European hat.

Before children are invested with the

sacred shirt and cord, their general holiday attire is a silk or satin dress, composed of a single piece, extending from the neck to the ankles, with a slit at the throat to permit of its being thrown with facility over the head. Wherever the means occur, these little dresses are handsomely embroidered with the floss of silk, and not unfrequently with bullion. The head-dress is a sort of hussar cap, embroidered with either gold or silver lace, in a manner peculiar to the country, fanciful, and not inelegant. So great is this passion for the decoration of their offspring, that even gold ornaments of great value are often arranged about their persons, in the form of necklets, bracelets, anklets, noselets with some valuable gem, and ear-rings also provided with pearls, emeralds, or other precious gems. Very frequently Pársí lads, until of the age of sixteen, wear rings either in one or both of their ears. Though Pársís take particular pride in extravagantly adorning their children, the most fastidious European eye would not take offence at their costume, unless it be an apprehension of dread for the cupidity which would desire the costly ornaments that are shown to such advantage. The poorest Pársí woman never ventures out of her house without a silk *sádí*, the outer dress of the sex, composed of several yards, first received in folds about the waist, and then thrown over the head, so that the outer end of the sádí falls upon the right arm. Precisely like the men, the women wear the kustí, sadrá, and drawers: without the two former they would not be Zerdusthíans.

Pársí ladies are intrusted wholly with the economy of the household, in which the men are not allowed to interfere. They are said to be thrifty, precise, and provident. They contrive to be perfectly conversant with the affairs of their relatives, so as to provide for themselves in times of danger and difficulty. Women of the tribe residing at Surát are dexterous in embroidery, particularly in floral designs in floss to the hems of the sádí of their countrywomen, and those of the pyjámá. Of late the Pársí ladies of Bombay have betaken themselves to wool-work, and a variety of European amusements and tastes, to fill up their leisure hours. The principal advance in civilisation is with the males, who are constantly abroad. Their women, certainly, are not now so confined to the house as was the custom formerly: they are even permitted to go abroad in open carriages, which was quite unusual so late as fifteen years ago. English hosiery has been in use among the better classes of both sexes for some years, and the men have a weakness in displaying fine English shoes, according to the season of the year. These innovations have been gradual, but are sensibly apparent.

With respect to the education of their females, it ought to be more generally known that most of them can both read and write the Gujarátí. The Students' Literary Society, to its credit, has of late seen to the establishment of schools and competent teachers for the better instruction of the sex. A few families among the wealthy have permitted their daughters to acquire a knowledge of English, and of those accomplishments cultivated by Europeans. Foremost to destroy the prejudice which had prevailed against so highly benevolent a purpose, was the late lamented Shet Frámjí Káuvasjí, in the education of his daughter, Phírozbái, stated many years ago in evidence given by the late Captain Cogan, of the Indian Navy, before a Parliamentary Committee. Then the Pársí Knight and Shet Mánakjí Karshedjí, names familiar to the public of Western India, and others not so well known who have done as much. Several Pársí ladies are said to manage the houses of agency conducted in the names of their husbands, and several widows wholly control the mercantile establishments bequeathed to them. The women of the Pársís are loquacious beyond belief, and their vocabulary of terms and compliments is, most assuredly, not the most choice. The men, with all their intercourse among Europeans, painful to add, are not much better. It is to be hoped that another generation will evince some taste on this score.

However narrow the pecuniary means of a Pársí, he will contrive to obtain for his sons a knowledge of the rudiments of Gujarátí, and, if he can endeavour it, education in English follows. For this purpose the Elphinstone Institution is a noble foundation, and the Pancháyat Charitable School a valuable auxiliary. The Gujarátí in use among the Pársís has been sadly corrupted by a copious employment of Persian phraseology, and as liberal an adoption of English words. The spirit of improvement leads the better educated youth to make English the chief medium of communication. Many of the Pársís speak and write English with a facility scarcely credible for foreigners. Ardeshír Behrámjí, the first Pársí interpreter in the Supreme Court of Bombay, published, in 1824, a Gujarátí grammar, to facilitate the progress of English students in acquiring that tongue. Sohorabsháh Dosabhái has published idiomatical exercises in

Gujarátí and English. Hírjíbhái and Meherwanjí, of the Láují family, who visited England, have furnished the public with a volume in English as to their impressions of England and its people. Náurosjí Firdunjí, one of the present Interpreters in the Queen's Court in Bombay, conducted for a length of time a scientific magazine in Gujarátí, called the *Vídhíya Sáugar*. Some of the Pársís are intimately conversant with Persian. Sohorabjí, the youngest son of Sir Jemshedjí Jijibhái, lately issued a translation of a Persian work into the Gujarátí dialect. A rising young merchant of Bombay, Shet Dhanjíbhái Frámjí, has devoted upwards of eight years to the compilation of a work on the Zend and Pehleví dialects, which he is about to publish. Munshí Dosabhái Sohorabjí has published idiomatical exercises in the Persian, Híndusthání, and Gujarátí languages, with corresponding lessons in English. Both he and his sons have their time fully engaged with students who desire to acquire the first three languages.

Of late years there have been several Pársís as probationer apprentices in the government hospitals, and some have been promoted as dressers in the service. The establishment of the Grant Medical College has led some respectable young men to graduate there, and who now have a fair practice among their countrymen. Half a dozen newspapers,* published in the Gujarátí dialect, are circulated among the Pársí community. Their alleged purpose is the publicity of useful information, and to promote a desire for intellectual and sound practical knowledge; but, it must be remarked, that their standard of taste is low, that they indulge in rancorous language, and are given to personalities—in one instance said to be carried on for years as a profitable speculation.

Pársís are notoriously given to good living. The best of flesh, fish, and fowl are whipped from a bazaar for their consumption: pork

* Appendix A.

and beef are their aversion, but mutton hams are imported by some of the gentry for their use. Every description of European wine is drunk. In the making up of their victuals the Pársís are rather gross, as they use large quantities of clarified butter, commonly known as *ghí*. Confectionery of every variety is largely partaken of, and bread after the English fashion is eaten by almost every member of the tribe. The Pársí commences the day by eating a light breakfast, often no more than a slice or two of bread, and of several cups of tea, which he drinks off with a handkerchief applied to the piece of pottery. His dinner is between twelve and two o'clock during the day, and is served in polished plates of brass; large quantities of rice are then consumed with curry, along with a variety of pungent ingredients, ground into what is called *chitní*, stews, &c. By tradesfolk, and the better classes of the community, a cup or more of tea is partaken of either at four or five o'clock in the afternoon. The evening meal occurs between eight and ten o'clock, when licence is given not only to beverages of variety and strength, but to the use of libidinous speech. The *tát* is the great parting dose of the night, not unlike the English stirrup-cup of yore, and the more recent Scottish form of "auld-lang-syne."

The bent of the Pársí mind is purely commercial. Many of their number have thus acquired wealth, position, and renown from the most obscure employment. The writer has been enabled to trace more than one who has commenced life as a *cuisinier*, or the butler of a household. Many years ago, it is said, there was a Pársí, who was so thoroughly conversant with navigation as to take the command of a vessel that plied between Penang and Siam. Now there are no soldiers, no sailors, porters, cobblers, tailors, smiths, tinkers, bricklayers, nor tilers; the occupations which principally engross notice are as merchants, bankers, shipwrights, upholsterers, brokers, ship-chandlers, money-changers, tavern-keepers, schoolmasters, bakers, and confectioners; shop-keepers, army contractors, clerks or English copyists, butlers in English families, coach-makers, coachies, auctioneers, *bandárís* or drawers of the *tádí*, turban-makers, watch-makers or rather repairers of watches, printers, weavers, agriculturists, cooks, apothecaries, vendors of millinery, and a few are attached to the Survey Department under Government.

Independent of those diseases of a climatarchic character, the liver complaint, dropsy, scrofula, and elephantiasis, Pársís, from their peculiar gross manner of living, are subject to sloughy ulcerous sores, which defeat the skill of the medical faculty, and their coarse skin renders surgical operation difficult and trying. Cutaneous complaints are not uncommon among them, and rare instances offer of albinos.

The morals of the very best of the Pársís are not of the highest possible standard. This arises from education, and their own peculiar habits and manners, and which only time and discipline can correct. Those of their number who have mixed among Europeans endeavour to be careful in pledging their word in transactions of any kind; otherwise they have studied the address and the courtesy of the European, without acquiring that fine sense of honour, and that genuine philanthropy, which mark the gentleman from the far west. A mere promise goes for the promise, without any knowledge of the moral obligation which accompanies; hence, much of the contumely that is thrown upon the Pársí community is undeserved, simply for a want of knowing better.

It has also been urged that the Pársí is libidinously disposed: this has been urged generally, and to which, of course, exceptions will and must offer. He is also given to gambling, and to many of those vices peculiar even to the most civilized of the human race. Comparatively, the records of Her Majesty's Supreme Court of Judicature can cite fewer instances of crimes against members of the

Zerdusthían creed than any other class of the population of Bombay. In fact, as a body, the Pársís are not only peaceably disposed, but favourably disposed to the British Government, and to regard the laws of that Government. Several Pársís have been transported to Singapore for different periods of time, for felonies of various kinds. Nearly half a century ago it is stated the first Pársí was hanged under the English law. Not many years ago a most ferocious murder was committed in broad daylight by a Pársí upon a fellow-countryman. In the noted Coal-conspiracy case, Karshedjí Meherwánjí Pátel was imprisoned for two years, and mulcted, in addition, in the sum of twenty thousand rupees. Vagabonds will be found among every community, and the Pársís rather offer an example of the small amount of crime that may be committed among the ethnic subjects of any Crown. Pársís are not only averse to committing suicide, but, until lately, entertained a prejudice against *post-mortem* examinations, which the law most properly overruled. Yet, not long ago, a Gujarátí newspaper broadly asserted that perjury was common to the Pársís, and that formerly they were in the habit of making away with women by poison, and by other subtle agencies.

SECTION III.

Religion.—The Magi who followed the Star of Bethlehem—Singular Inconsistencies in the Observance of certain Forms—Liturgical Works—Temples—Priesthood—Naming of Infants, &c.—Ceremony upon Marriage and at Death—Division among the Pársís—Days of the Month, &c.—Holidays.

THE speculative genius of the age may decide whether the Jannes and Jambres of Biblical writ are to be confounded with the authors of that form of Bhudism now prevalent in Western India as Jáinaism, or are to be recognised as of the same class as the Magi who worshipped the starry host of heaven, and, by this Sabian mode of faith, pursued that star of the east which rose with the birth of Jesus Christ, and induced them to offer myrrh and frankincense at his cradle,—the homage only due to royalty and divinity,—ample recognition of Him who came as a Prince and a Redeemer to the fallen sons of men. That these Magi were Persians, of that nation who are said to be the progenitors of the modern Pársís, not a doubt is now entertained by those capable of expressing an opinion on the subject.

Whatever the wisdom or morality contained in the sacred writing of the Pársís, disguised in the obsolete characters of the Zend and Pehleví, polemical disputants have ably argued so as to decide unfavourably to the integral character of the faith. Whatever the mission, personal efforts, and imputed morality of the author of their religious code, Zoroaster, or Zerdusht,—Gibbon, the historian of the Decline and Fall of the Roman Empire, at once the carping and the credulous, has ably set at rest. Sir William Jones, too, in his letter to M. Anquetil du Perron, playfully, pungently, and yet truly, exhibits the vague absurdities attempted to be upheld in the Zend Avesta. The only two Pársís who in recent times have devoted any serious attention to their spiritual works, have been the respective heads of the Mubed sections of the *Kadímís* and *Rasamis*—Mullah Firuz and Edal Dáru, both of whom have been dead some years now. Mullah Firuz is prominently named in Sir John Malcolm's work as having visited Persia for the purpose of recovering those ancient books of the community which may have got astray. Dr Wilson, in an able work both for research and controversial acumen, has entered largely upon the merits of the Pársí religion; and critically treated all those volumes, acknowledged by the tribe as appertaining to their faith, or the peculiar observances enjoined by it. The Pársís deny that they are pyrolatrously disposed, yet the sacred fire is preserved with grateful veneration in their temples; and the first flickerings of a flame at eventide are watched and saluted with some pious ejaculation. The Pársís repudiate a worship of the elements, the sun, the moon, and all the celestial orbs, yet they own them as merciful accessaries to the enjoyment of life, and, as such, worthy the praise and the blessings of mankind. A fanciful philanthropy may indulge in numberless caprices with the learned, but will the ignorant so regard matters? The evidence of Basil Hall during his stay at Bombay will be precisely the same with any observer of the present day. Hundreds of Zerdusthians may be seen on the Esplanade of Bombay in the cool of the afternoon, mumbling the Gujarátised Zend jargon of devotion, without a knowledge of what they utter, or the capacity to appreciate the observance undergone. Whatever may be urged by individual members of the community—as a body, the Pársís neither study their faith, nor do they much regard its practice. A leaning to European manners, and, happier still, a thirst for European knowledge, is rapidly wearing away ancient prejudices, and paving a glorious course for a coming generation. Since the celebrated fire in Bombay in 1802, when the larger portion of the buildings in that portion of the Fort occupied by natives was destroyed, the Pársís have notoriously assisted in quenching fire: not only in Bombay, but this has been witnessed both at Calcutta and in China—at the former, from the testimony of Mr Bailie Fraser; and at the latter, the writer has learned of several credible eye-witnesses. Pársís are said to entertain scruples, not only about putting out a flame, or fire in any form, but to use fire-weapons of any kind; yet the writer has seen one Pársí fire off a pistol, and happens to be aware of another who has been engaged in a duel, and carries to this day the brand of his opponent's bullet. Pársís are said not to take their women to any locality where there is neither *átesh behrám* or *dokma*, or where *ínjání* has not been performed; yet they are to be found, even in the province of Gujarát, scores of miles away from either fire-temple or tower of silence. A number of Pársís have been buried at Macao without the city walls, and have tombs after the Anglican form, with inscriptions, bearing the names and other particulars of the parties, both in English and in Gujarátí. So many startling inconsistencies occur among the Pársís themselves regarding their own pristine hallowed rites and tenets, that the progress of innovation promises to eradicate them wholly, rather than to encourage their continuance, even partially. One fanciful exception offers,—granting that the cow is not worshipped, and knowing it to be the vestige of one of the numerous Híndu customs adopted by the Pársís. Even the credulity of Sir William Jones affects fastidiousness as to the use of *l'urine de bœuf*,—yet the elegant and dashing, the good, learned, grave, delicate, and pious—all, equally, rinse the mouth, and anoint the eyes and tips of the ears with this material as a matutinal ceremony. No curious investigator into the customs of the followers of Zerdusht will have omitted to notice the brass *lota*, or pot, employed for this purpose after the sun has risen. Strange as what has been already observed may appear, the subject is deserving notice, and this the writer will endeavour to do more gravely.

The Pársís were permitted a settlement in Híndusthán upon an assurance of conforming to certain customs. Very soon—whether arising from inclination, the indolent acquiescence to usages engendered by peculiarity of climate, or constant intercourse with the natives of the new country, the political necessity, or by way of compliment to the lords of the land—they adopted, along with the rights and tenets of Zerdusht, the ceremonial services current among Híndus at seasons of marriage and death, independent of the courtesies of ordinary life, and the outer attire now worn. The Pársís became as superstitious as the people around them, and, like the Hebrews of old, sought strange gods. They resorted to the temples of Jāina and Brāhmanical worship, as well as the superstructures of Muslim faith; and in later times, also, vowed for earthly aggrandizement at the Church of the Christian. Even now it is very little better. The Pársí community, too, do not appear to have been ignorant of these evils; and its Pancháyat at Bombay, in November 1819, issued a manifesto of sundry pains and penalties upon *women* —matters had gone this length—who should be found frequenting the *derās*, or shrines, of Mambá Deví, Bhulesvár, Máhá Laksmí, Vālkesvar, or attend the Hulí for throwing cocoa nuts into the fire; or permit their infants, in the company or charge of other individuals to proceed to any Híndu fane for the purpose of making or performing any vows or ceremonies,—extending this prohibition equally to the haunts of Muhammadan devotion, and to the celebration, even in their dwelling-houses, of the *Chathí*, *Kandal*, and *Hazírat*; and, moreover, to the use of threads, charms, amulets, or phylacteries, obtained of magicians. Apparently with a view of giving a more legitimate tone and character to their matrimonial and funeral services, the Pancháyat proceeded more gravely in their deliberations; and one of its leading members, aided by his colleagues, framed a code, for the guidance of the Gabars, which was formally submitted to the general assembly of the sect, at a public meeting held at Shet Dadabhái Nasarvanjí's *Ateshbehram*, or chief fire-temple, on the 18th of October 1823, when and where the code was formally recognised. Yet, the Pársí will still continue to form a vow, and present his offering at the altar of Nossa Senora de Monte, at Bandurá, in Salset; and it would be an endless effort to proceed in illustration of this point. What, in Surat, for instance, is more Híndu-like than the divesting the face of hair upon a death in the family? What more Muhammadan than the superstitious vagaries by which he permits himself to be beset—independent of the evil spirits by which he is allowed to be annoyed by Ahríman, the evil genius of his destiny and his faith? and repugnant as all this may appear to his ordinary professions, what shall be urged for his interest in the canine species? Pársís do not hold that tenderness to animal-life which the Bhudists of this part of the Indian peninsula entertain—yet the dog-riot, which occurred at Bombay in 1832, was mainly occasioned by the Pársís. Mr Henry Gray was violently assaulted by some members of their community when driving into town in an open carriage: provisions of any kind could not be obtained by Europeans for two or three days previously; and, ultimately, a detachment of H. M.'s 2d Regiment of Foot, or Queen's Royals, had to be called into the Fort of Bombay from Colaba, to quell the disturbance, when assuming a serious aspect. Pársís do value the canine species, but merely for the absolving character attributed to their vision when meeting that of a dying mortal! This sight is denominated *chár chasham*, or quadrupled gaze. Effectually to accomplish such a purpose, curds are planted on the forehead immediately between the eyebrows; and the brute, in licking the curds, affords the dying creature his purpose. Ridiculous as this may seem, and scouted as it is by the respectable portion of the community, it is nevertheless well known throughout Gujarát.

The great work of the Zerdusthians is the ZEND AVESTA, or Zend Word, which comprises the *Vandídád*, said to be very loosely translated by M. du Perron; the *Yaçna*, or Izashne, also translated into French by M. Eugéne Burnouf; the *Khurdah Avasta*, and several subsidiary sections appertaining to the inferior offices enjoined by the faith. Both the Yaçna and Vandídád Sade, in the Zend dialect but Gujarátí characters, have been published in a lithographed form by Frámjí Aspandiárjí, under the direction of Mullah Fíruz, and other learned Andhíarus of the Kadímís; it is accompanied by a Gujarátí translation, paraphrase, and comment, according to the traditional interpretation of the Zerdusthians. In this form the Vandídád was presented to the public in 1842, and the Yaçna in the year following. An English translation of M. Perron's labours is about to be committed to the press by a Pársí gentleman, with emendations and annotations. Dr Wilson has entered into an erudite critique on this work. The Zerdusthians' history of their spiritual lawgiver is contained in the *Zertusht-Namah*, a traditional narrative in verse of Zertusht; which has been translated by Lieutenant E. B. Eastwick, of the Bombay Army.

But, as has been already asserted, whatever the character and merits of this faith,—sealed as it is to general acquaintance from the peculiar characters—in other words, the dead languages—in which they have been written and continue to be preserved, they exist rather as historical figments than as records of their peculiar tenets and devotional exercises. The subject has successfully engaged the attention of able men, interested in an acquaintance with their writings from the noblest and holiest of purposes; and no Pársí, whatever his pretensions, would attempt to dispute the opinion Mr Erskine pronounced upon the intrinsic merits of their spiritual philosophy, however prejudiced their present impressions against Dr Wilson.

The consecrated hall of worship of the Zerdusthian, from familiarity of expression, is now known as *Agherí*, a compound Gujarátí word signifying, literally, "fire-house." The more correct terms, and those popular among the sect, are *Atesh-Behrám*, *Atesh-Adharán*, and *Atesh-Dhádagáhá*. The first of these appellations is equivalent in character to the Episcopalian Cathedral. *Behrám* and *Adharán* are the descriptions of sacred fire. The first of these is deemed more holy, from the one thousand and one sources from which it is derived, and is said to exist only in nine of their temples in India; and the second, which is more largely scattered, has but seven sources. Sir Henry Pottinger, in his travels through Beluchísthán, makes mention of the *Atesh-Kudu*, said to exist in some subterraneous fane in Persia.

The Pársís still remember, from traditional story, the circumstance of M. Anquetil du Perron and his companion's stay at Surat. They are the only Europeans known and acknowledged to have entered into their temples. The legend, for such it now is, current among them is, that two Mubeds from Persia resided among them for some years. They wore the attire and in every other way conformed to the usages of Zerdusthians; they were perfectly familiar with their religious rites and liturgical services. Only upon Perron's return to Europe, the Pársís became aware of these foreigners having duped them. At Surat the Pársís have two temples. At Náusárí, eighteen miles to the south-west of Surat, Sir Jemshedjí Jijíbhái has recently had erected a massive construction, with stone conveyed from Bombay, independent of the one built in 1765; at Gandave, twenty-seven miles in the same direction from Surat, Shet Jemshedjí Wádíyá has built one; at Ahmedábád, built by public subscription; at Puná, in the Dekhan, another foundation of the benevolent Pársí knight; and at Calcutta, one built by the late Shet Rustomjí Kauvasjí, an opulent merchant, long connected with the City of Palaces. The most ancient edifice of the community is at Udhawádá, twenty-seven miles to the south-west and by west of Surat, built by Anjumán of Sanján, A. D. 720, not long after the arrival of the Zerdusthians on that coast of India. At the seat of the Presidency of Bombay the first temple was erected at the expense of Dádábhái Nasarwánjí, some time in 1781; it belongs to the Kadímís. The more popular temple appertaining to the Rasamí division was consecrated at the cost of the late Shet Hormasjí Bahmanjí, of the Wádíyá family, in 1830. Both these come under the denomination of *Atash-Behram*, are in the Sunápur division of the island, and occupy the right and left, almost opposite each other, of the road to Girgaum. There are four inferior temples in the Fort, and a good number of them in different parts of Bombay, where any number of the community may have settled.

The Levitical section of the Pársí community is said to remain as pure in blood, and intact in constitution, as the first emigrants from the soil of their ancestors. They are debarred marrying without the pale of the section. A priest remains virtually a priest for ever, and is only permitted to ally himself among the families of the priesthood. He is at liberty, however, to engage in traffic or other employment, but in doing so he is not allowed to perform any of the sacerdotal offices. Excepting these, all engaged upon the rites of their creed wear a white turban, as distinctive of the Mubed from the Behdín. *Mubed* is the general term, and tantamount in acceptation to our word clergy; the learned among them, and those who hold spiritual dignity, are denominated *Dasturs*, or *Andhíárus*, almost significant to our Doctors and Bishops; *Herbads* are the inferior clergy, and *Nasar-sálás* are criers, and carriers of the funeral bier. Yet so fastidious is the prejudice of the tribe, that a Mubed will avert his face from a Nasar-sálá if he should gain a sight of him, and absolutely refuse all intercourse with him, unless he has undergone the process of purification, and then *only* will he condescend to salute or to eat with him. According to the circumstances of the laity, every family supports from one to half-a-dozen such professional gentlemen, and upon particular occasions the benevolence of their friends is put to the test. The Pársís even acknowledge, with some degree of sorrow, that the Mubed section of their community no longer contains any men of ability, or who promise talent; and too frequently the priest of a household, while made the confidant of the women, is the butt and buffoon of the men—though the necessary ceremonies are performed with all that pleasure entertained by a patient in swallowing the nauseous draught prescribed by his physician.

The first occasion that a Mubed's offices are put in requisition is upon the birth of a child. The Pársís denounce astrology, and yet are fiercely superstitious; they despise the absurd customs engendered by Brahminism, and yet conform to many of them: one such now offers. The moment birth is given to a child—say a male—his horoscope is consulted; the peculiar planet under which his nativity has occurred, and certain corresponding types are then traced upon a tabular record, which furnishes the first letter of the names to be given him, whether પ *p* or ફ *ph*—Pestan or Fráma, and so on. The next occasion is upon investiture with the sacred *kustí*, or cincture, consisting of seventy-two interwoven filaments required to circumvent the waist three times; and the *sadra*, or shirt, emblematic of that panoply which protects its wearer from Ahriman, the Evil Principle. The precise time this should take place is when the child happens to be seven years, seven months, and ten days old; but in wealthy families this ceremony is performed much earlier, to permit of an infantile nuptial covenant, and the ceremony is repeated at the given time. Instances occur frequently where the investiture is postponed in consequence of the penurious circumstances of the parents. In alluding to children, it might be mentioned that a strange custom prevails with the Pársís as to the necessity for a woman giving birth to her child on the ground-floor of a house; and if she should be taken with the pains of travail at the topmost story of a house of several stories, she is conveyed instantly below. For forty days after giving birth, the female is kept apart from the household. All the trifling pageantry popular among Híndus upon the marriage of children, and its never-failing expense, also exists among Pársís. In only two instances have Pársís permitted their daughters marrying at the years of puberty, and these have happened in the families of Mánakjí Karshedjí and Sir Jemshedjí Jíjíbhái,—the same gentlemen who have been already named as having bestowed upon their daughters an European education. The matrimonial ceremony consists in the bride and bridegroom being seated close to each other with their right hands clasped, the relatives holding a handkerchief between them so as to prevent their seeing each other; and while the priest performs the liturgical service for the occasion, a thread is carried several times round the chairs of the contracting parties. This is the most important feature of the proceeding, and occurs before any of the parade already noticed. Bigamy has been tolerated among the Pársís, and no law exists for its prevention. Pársí widows, unlike Híndus, are permitted to re-marry. Sometimes a black *sádí* is worn for a few months, but the actual state of widowhood is only recognised by the ornaments about the female's person being destroyed at the time, an act generally confined to the bracelets;—ornaments not being resumed until a second marriage. Upon the approaching death of a member of the Pársí community, the body is brought on the ground-floor: so soon as pulsation is lost its ablution occurs, and not unfrequently the limbs are disjointed so far as to render them loose, and readily detached. The wrists are now tied by a ribbon, and not unfrequently the ankles,—the body is then wrapped in its nude condition in a clean white cotton sheet, and placed upon an iron skeleton-frame. The body is not allowed to remain in the house any length of time; and the more scrupulous parties have it removed by a side, in preference to the usual general entrance. The carriers of the bier have their hands, feet, and head bound in white cloth. Two sets generally accompany, so as to permit of changes at intervals on the road to the *dokma*, or tower of silence. The followers of a funeral procession proceed in couples, holding a handkerchief between them; they are otherwise in full-dress, that is to say,—the *jhámá* is worn. The cortege is always *sur le pied.* Upon the body being introduced into the *dokma* by the required orifice, and the performance of the *satom*, or service for the dead, the friends and mourners disperse; while, according to the garrulous, the nasar-sálás remain to watch the particular eye torn from its socket by vultures, and other birds of carrion, who pounce upon the carcase, and from this is ascertained the bliss or misery endured by the spirit once animating it. Both the *dokmas* of the tribe at Bombay are upon Malabar Point; one has existed for more than a century, and the more modern erection was open to the public before its consecration some fifteen years ago. Peculiar as is this custom to the Pársís, like the Chinese, they entertain a grateful veneration for the manes of their forefathers, for whose happiness in the world of spirits they have a large collection of prayers. Withal, excepting the *nasar-sálás*, neither Mubed nor Behdín are permitted to approach a *dokma* within seventy-two feet, when he would have to perform the ceremonies enjoined for purification.

The great *Kabísah* (intercalary month) controversy relative to the computation of their year, or the era of Yezdijírd, led to the existing division among the Pársís in the early portion of the last century. The difference appears to have originated in Persia, where the Sul-i-Kadím was then current, which commenced a month earlier than with the system popular among the Pársís in India. The individual of their community who proceeded to Persia to ascertain the occasion of this difference, happened to be of the profession of a *Churígar*, or bracelet-maker; and, as he held the same view as the Zerdusthians in Persia, those in India partaking of the like impression were denominated *Churígaríyán*, or *Kadímí*, from the era; those retaining the original form of chronology current among them, comprising the major portion of the tribe, were, from contrast, called *Rasami*, or "customary," and *Shaher-sáhí*, signifying "city-like," or ironically as the "black-faced." Recently it has been attempted to modify this last sobriquet into *Sháhansháhi*, or "King-of-kings,"—from a municipal to an imperial character. This is the only real division among the Pársís, and the holidays and festivals of the Rasamí and Kadímí in consequence differ a month in every year. The family of Dádí Shet and the Banájís are the great supporters of the Kadímís; and to this section also belonged the late Mullah Firuz.

The *Sífat-í-Sirozah* furnishes the necessary detail regarding the *Roze-sí-o-se*, or thirty days of each month, over which a particular angel of bliss presides. The days fall in the following order, and the particular office of these several spirits in heaven is given in the *Manahájáth*, a Persian word, implying the "adoration of angels":—

1. Hormazd.
2. Behman.
3. Ardebehísht.
4. Sherívar.
5. Ispandhármad.
6. Khurdád.
7. Amerdád.
8. Dhepádar.
9. Adar.
10. Abhán.
11. Khurshíd.
12. Máh, or Moher.
13. Thír.
14. Gosh.
15. Dhepmeher.
16. Meher.

17. Sarvosh or Serosh.
18. Rashne.
19. Farvardín.
20. Behrám.
21. Ram.
22. Gavád.
23. Dhepdín.
24. Dín.
25. Arshavasang, or Ashasang.
26. Asthád, or Ashtád.
27. Asmán.
28. Zamíadh.
29. Máharesphand.
30. Anírán.

From the foregoing, twelve names have been appropriated for the months in the following order:—1, Farvardín; 2, Ardebehísht; 3, Khurdád; 4, Thír; 5, Amerdád; 6, Sherívar; 7, Meher; 8, Abhán; 9, Adar; 10, Dhe; 11, Behman; 12, Ispandhármad. When the *Máhí* (month) and *Roze* (day) of the first month come together—in other words, the day Farvardín of the month Farvardín is regarded as a *Jasne* or *Parab*, and hence its being significantly denominated Farvardhíyán; the same with Thír—hence Thíríyán; Meher, Meheríyán; Abhán, Abhánu; Adar, Adáru; and Behman also known as Goshpand. In the month of Farvardín and roze Adar occurs another Parab, called Adar Farvardín. In all seven Parabs or Jasne. With the months of Ardebehísht and Khurdád they are known as Humkáre. Nothing occurs on the occasion of Amerdád, Sherívar, and Ispandhármad. Dhe has no roze whatever. To complete the solar year, the remaining five days which have neither month nor date, and hence denominated *Gáthá Gambárs*, are respectively known in the following order:—*Ahonuad*, *Oshthoad*, *Sepenthoad*, *Vohoshathre*, and *Vasthohasth*. These also bear an especial signification, as *Hamas-peth-madhem*, and the last *gáthá* is also called *Náuroz*. During these five days prayers are bountifully raised by Zerdusthíans for the spirits of the departed being released from their bonds to that state of purity to enable them to meet and protect their friends among the living. Independent of these, five other *Gambárs* occur during the year, and they are called *Medhío-zarm*, *Medhío-shahem*, *Petheshahem*, *I-á-thwem*, and *Medhí-arem*. The following fasts and festivals are observed by

Zerdusthians:—*Mukthád*, or *Doslá*, eleven days before the new year, when great ceremonies are performed for the souls of the dead; *Vachlímachí*, the 360th day of their year, and upon the following day falls the first of the Gáthá Gambárs, *Papatí*, or New-Year's Day; and *Khordadshal*. These are wholly sacred seasons. But the especial occasion of enjoyment, when mirth, and revelry, and riot are in full flow, is *Sulthaní Nauroz*, maintained in memory of their glorious King Jámshed. The five *Gambars* named occur in the following order:—

Medhío-zarm.—In the month of Ardebehísht, and on the day Khurshíd.

Medhío-shahem.—In the month of Thír, and on the day Khurshíd.

Pethe-shahem.—In the month of Sherívar, and on the day Asthád.

I-a-thwem.—In the month of Meher, and on the day Asthád.

Medhí-arem.—In the month of Dhe, and on the day Meher.

The following occasions are allowed in all public offices as holidays—they occur in the order given, viz. :—Jámshed Náuroz, one day; Jasne Abán, one day; Jasne Adár, one day; Jasne Farvardín, one day; the five Gáthá Gambárs; *Papatí*, or New-Year's Day; Khordádshal, one day; and Atash-behrám Sálgherí, or anniversary of the great fire, one day,—in all, thirteen days in the year.

SECTION IV.

The Panchâyat.

IN their exode from that land which had seen at once their rise, their renown, and their ruin, the Zerdusthians, while attempting to preserve their sacred literature, wholly lost that code of domestic legislature which had been their means of guidance. Broken by reverses, or perhaps pining in exile, the early Pársís who sought refuge at the north-western coast of the peninsula of Híndusthán were unequal to the effort, or doubted the necessity of preserving, what they at least knew of such observances; they became thus lost to their descendants: but separated, as a tribe by blood, and in peculiarity of faith, from the surrounding people, so soon as they gathered in force, they formed, from the worth, wealth, and talent of their community, a *Panchá-*

yat, or assembly of five, which was afterwards extended in number, towards protecting their creed from innovations, and guarding their peculiar traditions. This assembly partook more of the character of the Jewish Sanhedrim than the Venetian Council of Ten; it possessed to all intents and purposes, with the voluntary consent of the tribe, its due constitutional government, without affecting the political relations of the sovereign in whose country they dwelt, and whose subjects they became. All the great questions of the Pársís were to be mooted only in an *Agherí*, and in that *Agherí* only every individual was permitted freely to tender his expressions thereon. The meeting was convened by the *Nasarsálá*, or crier, under the injunctions of the Pancháyat, communicating at the same time the nature of the propositions to be then submitted. On such occasions, also, occurred the elections of the members of the Panchá-yat as casualties befell, or the necessity demanded, but from two to four only of their number exercised the functional offices attendant upon the appointment—in counselling, appeasing domestic feuds, and the other arrangements consequent upon such a position. Peace, unanimity of purpose, and justice, appear to have been the intentions of such an institution; and they were worthy the descendants of those who owned the rule of Cyrus. Towards the close of the last century, and owing to the increasing number and respectability of the Pársí community, the Bombay Government selected twelve of the Pancháyat, with a view that they should have the determination of all causes of dispute among their own class. Like the flickerings of a flame, which are always brightest and boldest when near extinction, so with the association under notice. Hitherto it had gathered in conclave, proposed, abolished, provided, pacified, and punished, as circumstances deemed expedient, by mere *vivâ voce* arrangement; there was no digest of their particular customs, and their observances;

and suddenly, affected by the imperative need for such *bandubastas*, a great demonstration was accomplished by the meeting at the Agherí of Shet Dádábhái Nasarvanjí, of the whole of the Pancháyat, on the 4th March 1818. It was composed of twelve *Behdíns*, two *Dasturs*, and four *Mubeds*. The subject which at the time engaged their especial notice was the progress of bigamy among their community, and the necessity of arresting that progress; and, with this view, they had now resolved "that nobody who has a wife living shall marry another." For some five years afterwards this tribunal continued to maintain the reputation it had gained, for the wholesome and salutary effects of its decisions; and then, whether through disagreements among its body, or the presence of party spirit, there was a relaxation in the tone it had hitherto upheld, and a number of irregularities were indolently permitted.

Perhaps a more important obstacle operated upon its character as a municipal element. Upon the establishment of the Recorder's Court at Bombay, it was provided by the Charter granted to it, that in all actions and suits of Muhammadans and *Gentoos*,—a very vague definition, and which would have been equally applicable to Pársís from the manner in which it was employed by the Portuguese, who coined it as a general appellation for the Natives of Hindusthan, but which was understood to be strictly applied to Hindus,—that they should be determined by their own laws and usages. The absence of any direct mention of the Pársís in the Charter led litigants of their community interested in estates to interpret—"that, as Pársís were neither Hindus nor Muhammadans, the inheritance and succession to lands, rents, and goods, should be determined according to English law." An appeal was made, in consequence, to the Governor General and Legislative Council, for an enactment "to quiet the possession of estates already acquired by Pársís in the way of succession, and to fix the law by which the succession to the estates of Pársís, either by inheritance or testamentary disposition, is to be regulated in future." This appeal was numerously signed, under date the 20th November 1835: it was only transmitted through the legitimate channel— the Government of Bombay—on the 23d March following; and while it met with the favourable notice of the Government of India, it was not replied to before the 30th of January 1837. A little better than two months afterwards the Pársís of Bombay expressed their acquiescence in the terms of the proposed enactment, and it was promulgated by the Right Honourable the Governor General of India on the 15th May 1837, and as Act No. IX. of that year. Both the correspondence and Act are furnished in the Appendix.* Pushing their intentions towards the recognition of certain prescribed privileges peculiar to their community, the

* Vide B.

Pársís again addressed the Supreme Government on the 21st November 1838, submitting, at the same time, a series of questions put by Mr Harry Borradaile, of the Bombay Civil Service, at the time Judge of Surat,—a gentleman who had bestowed some attention to the ancient languages and literature of the Zerdusthians,—and their replies thereto, in compliance with such customs arising from tradition, and recognised by the more respectable members of their community. It was not simply seeking the establishment by the authorities of their usages with respect to inheritance, but the memorial insidiously employed this means towards the recognition of the Pancháyat as the lawgivers, and the tribunal of punishment and reward of their countrymen. The appeal was tacitly permitted to lay aside, and the Pársís never endeavoured to resuscitate the subject—mainly from the unconcern evinced by the authorities towards acknowledging such an assembly as the Pancháyat. Long prior, however, to the Government being memorialized relative to Pársí inheritances, Shet Bohmanjí Hormasdjí Wádíyá placed himself in communication with Sir John Wither Awdry, the Puisné Justice of H. M.'s Supreme Court at Bombay, on the subject of the paper got up in conjunction with Mr Borradaile; Sir John very properly observes, "that the difficulty of framing a statute to that effect would be as little as can ever be expected in such cases, as the whole appears to be a very sensible and coherent system." Mr Justice Awdry's letter also forms part of the Appendix. Yet this subject of Pársí inheritance had been mooted nearly some thirty years before in the Recorder's Court, and during the time of Sir James Mackintosh. The case was that of the well-known Ghístás family, which involved large and valuable properties. Upon the conflicting and abnegatory evidence—"flatly contradicting each other," is the expression of one of their own number—of several respectable Pársís, the erudite Recorder pronounced judgment, that according to the tenets and customs enjoined by the Zerdusthian persuasion, bastards, when even begot by strange women of other nations, upon being invested with their sacred badge, ceased to be considered illegitimate; and, under the circumstances, permitted a natural son the right of heirship to his father's estate. A singular coincidence occurred at this time, which, viewed in whatever light—whether as to their vanity, their pretensions, or their true customs—reflects sorely on the Pársís. It is sufficiently well told by Shet Frámjí Káuvasjí, who was the party to the conference, and his own words are given as they are taken literally from the translation of a note appended to the notice served on the Pancháyat by Náurosji Jemshedjí Vádíyá of his resignation of the seat at their council, and under date the 8th of June 1836—"Mr John Leckie, who then was one of the sitting aldermen, sent for me, and told me that the Court had, in that case, allowed a Pársí illegitimate son to inherit his father's estate; consequently, in ten or twenty years there would exist no difference between the legitimate and illegitimate children, and that they all might be termed bastards alike; and that though Pársí gentlemen were well treated by Europeans, and allowed chairs to sit on, they would not hereafter be considered, under the above circumstances, respectable enough to be treated with even such common civilities! The case in question above-mentioned was subsequently brought to a new trial before Sir John Newbolt, and by rejecting former contradictory evidences he declared it as his opinion, and decreed it accordingly, that a Pársí illegitimate son is entitled to a life maintenance only, and nothing more, from his father's estate." Nor is it ascertained from the foregoing whether the force of custom or the dread of losing European notice operated to greater advantage in rendering the evidence less conflictory at a fresh suit, and towards acquiring the verdict then obtained.

But the Pancháyat of 1818, in their

opening *bandubast*, or manifesto, make the following declaration:—"After the death of those members (former, or preceding members), the people were in the habit of bringing their complaints before the sons of the said deceased members who were competent to hear them, and they were in the habit of hearing and deciding on the same. Many of the last individuals have since died, and the numbers of our people are every day increasing in Bombay, and several among them are transgressing our usages, and misleading others; therefore the whole Pancháyat have this day assembled together, and resolved that twelve Behdíns, and six Dasturs and Mubeds, making in all eighteen individuals, shall in future be competent, in case of dispute among our people, and on any complaint being preferred, to hear the complaint, and call the defendant before them, to hear their respective witnesses; and to decide the same in a proper manner. The names of the eighteen individuals thus appointed to the Pancháyat are as follow:—

" *Behdíns.*—Dávar Frámji Nánábhái,
Vádíyájí Náurosjí Jemshedji,
Shet Karshedjí Ardashírjí,
Dhanjíbhái Sohorábjí (*ready-money*),
Vádíyájí Hormasdji Bohmanjí,
Frámji Káuvasjí Banají,
Sohorábjí Váchá Ghándí,
Barjurjí Dohorábjí Dádí Barjorná,
Karshedjí Mánakjí Saráf,
Dádábhái Káuvasjí Sáiyar,
Pestanjí Bhíkájí Pándená, and
Náurosjí Meherjí.

" *Dasturs.*—Dasturjí Karshedjí Jemshedji, of Nausárí, and Mullah Pherosjí Kauvasjí.

" *Mubeds.*—Shet Meherwánjí Náurosjí,
Shet Rastumjí Sápurjí,
Panthítrí Dohorábjí Frámjí, and
Andhiáru Hormasjí Dohorábjí Laskarí.

"These have been duly appointed: but to obviate delay, which must take place in gathering all of them together in ordinary cases of dispute among our people, or on a complaint of a trifling nature being preferred—and as Vádíyáji Jemshedjí Bohmanjí, and Verá Frámjí Nánábhaí Ðávar were hitherto deciding such ordinary disputes, it is resolved that they shall continue to do so according to the rules of the Pancháyat; adding to their number, in cases where they should think proper, two or four other individuals from those abovenamed, and thus united afford redress to the petitioners; and their decision, when accepted by the parties, shall be approved of by the Pancháyat. But if any of the parties, after accepting such decision, decline to act in compliance therewith, he shall be punished by the Pancháyat according to the extent of his guilt.

"Further, if the party is dissatisfied with the decision of the two or four individuals, and should desire that the whole eighteen should be convened, or that ten or twelve from among them do so, to decide his case; or should he be desirous of having other members added to the said eighteen above-mentioned—in that event, six additional members may be nominated and the case proceeded with, and their verdict meet the approval of the Pancháyat; and any party refusing to abide by such decision, shall be punished by the Pancháyat to the full extent of his guilt.

"Further, should the complainant desire that his case be referred for the decision of the whole Pancháyat, then a general Pancháyat of young and old shall assemble and decide his case; and in the event of the eighteen or twenty-four individuals differing in opinion, and if the general assembly there met divide among themselves on the question, in such cases it is ordained that the decision of a majority of those gathered be considered as final, and shall be admitted accordingly; and any of the parties refusing to abide by the same, shall be punished by the Pancháyat according to the circumstances of his case."

Concluding this important *bandubast* with this paragraph:—"To the foregoing particulars have we all agreed, after having had the same previously read; and after having made ourselves acquainted with the same, and which we have now duly confirmed. Although this is signed by some, and not by others, it is binding on all now living in Bombay wearing '*the badge of Zerdusht,*' and those who may hereafter arrive and settle here; and those who shall not conform to the above rules, shall be punished by the Pancháyat as aforesaid."

The proceedings of this convention now bore a solemn and systematic impress; and the circumstance of conveying to paper the purposes of their deliberation led greater regularity to prevail than might heretofore have happened. An instance of many occurs immediately after the proceedings just noticed,—on the 2d July 1818, extracted from the minutes of that occasion:—

"That Andhiáru Hormasjí Dohorábjí, one of the eighteen appointed by the Pancháyat, having gone abroad on commercial affairs, without giving intimation thereof to the

Pancháyat, the Pancháyat congregated this day have, therefore, unanimously resolved to appoint Dastur Edaljí Dohorábjí Sahanjáná in room of the said Andhiaru Hormasjí Dohorábjí." Among other *notabilia* of the kind on its records, occurs under date the 15th of October 1823,—"That of those who held seats in the Pancháyat, Naurosjí Meherjí, and Pantháki Darabdáru Frámjí having departed this life, the assembly this day convened have appointed Jemshedjí Jíjíbhaí and Andhiaru Hormasdjí Dohorabjí in their places." The Pancháyat now proceeded towards enforcing very happy restrictions in the extravagance hitherto displayed at marriages, and the expenses incurred upon deaths; defining the *Asudád*, "gift to the pious," doled out previously to the clergy, and endeavouring to combat the growing taste for bigamy. This last appeared, and was felt, as the most heinous offence; but it grew out of a time-honoured (with the Pársís) Hindu ceremonial of betrothing and marrying children, almost in infancy. The first notice taken of a breach of the Pancháyat's decree happened not long after the great gathering of March 1818, and the delinquent was a wealthy man, connected too by relationship with one of the members of the Pancháyat, Jemshedjí Behramjí by name. He appears to have effected his second marriage, and during the lifetime of his first wife, at Udápura, in the contiguity of Surat. Nothing daunted by his purpose, he returned to Bombay, when the Pancháyat took an early occasion of meeting, and expelled him from the community of their tribe. Upon ascertaining that his father still afforded shelter to Jemshedjí, the Pancháyat, at a further sitting, came to the resolution of summoning the parent before their conclave; and insisted upon the expulsion of the son, at the cost of the father himself being excommunicated. Exasperated at this treatment, Jemshedjí employed opprobrious epithets to the Pancháyat, and assaulted its officiating priest. A complaint was in consequence preferred at the Police, and Jemshedjí, in expressing sorrow for his outrageous deportment, promised to abide by such punishment as the Pancháyat should award. The case came before that assembly on the 10th April of that year, while sitting in conclave at the Agherí of Dádí Shet: when it was decreed, quite in compliance it will be observed with Oriental custom,—"*That Jemshedjí should hold his own shoe in his hand, and with it beat himself over his face five times in presence of the Pancháyat, to be congregated for the purpose of witnessing it; and further, then and there to place a pátrá* (a piece of rough cloth) *round his neck and ask pardon, and to bear the expense of the lawyers, which the Pancháyat had to incur by going to law with him.*" This sentence, very humiliating and distressing as it must have been to Jemshedjí, was carried into execution on the 16th of June next. On the 2d of July, the Pancháyat, in considering the contents of several petitions presented them by Jemshedjí Behramjí, entreating forgiveness for his offence, and restitution to the rights of his countrymen, announced that Jemshedjí should humbly implore the pardon of the Pancháyat in public, where he should make his appearance with a *patká* round his neck, and immediately after undergo the humiliating process of purification, towards re-admission into the society; that he deposit the sum of two thousand rupees with the Pancháyat towards the maintenance of his first wife, restoring to her at the time all her jewellery and other property, and that he discharge to the Pancháyat the *Dhotí* (or cloth) fine. Jemshedjí's second wife was also obliged to go through the ceremony of purification, and to pay as well a *Dhotí* fine.

Another instance of Spartan determination of character transpired a few years afterwards. The Pancháyat had by proclamation abrogated an extravagant fashion which prevailed of circulating cooked dinners, with confectionery and fruit, on peculiar occasions following the death of a kinsman. A sister of one of the gentlemen of the Pancháyat very soon after violated this *bandubast*, and upon its gaining the ear of one of his colleagues, he instantly ordered the seizure of the dishes, without regard to the prominent situation of the town in which the order would be executed, or the umbrage it might give a distinguished family. So soon as the seizure was effected, a number of indigent Pársís were collected at an Agherí, where they were treated upon the feast, while the brass and silver plate were confiscated. Intimation was then made to the party whose relative had transgressed the Pancháyat's order, calling upon him at the same time to discharge his own important obligations to the assembly by making an example of the delinquent. The member of the Pancháyat instantly applauded the conduct of his colleague in the affair, consented to the meeting of the Pancháyat the very next day, when and where he expressed his marked disapprobation of the occurrence, and caused one of his erring sister's sons to pay on her behalf the *Dhotí* fine.

Alterations were, however, now in vogue; and a clever writer, a Pársí gentleman too, Shet Mánakjí Karshedjí, in summing the proceedings of past and present members of the Pancháyat, (in a series of letters addressed to a Bombay newspaper, under the signature of "*Q. in the Corner*,") very tersely observes:—"The former strove to maintain the sacred principle of treating the poor and rich alike, the latter were bent upon sacrificing that inestimable principle; the former were for assembling the Pancháyat, from time to time, in the usual manner, in one of their public places of worship, the latter could not bear the idea of having their measures openly canvassed by the public, and were for having instead, private meetings in their houses and offices; the former were for continuing to a class of Pársís, called *Pasthákíyás*, the privilege which they enjoyed for nearly half a century, of celebrating the first day of particular *gambars* by giving a feast to the whole community, while the latter were for conceding the privilege to one of their friends; the former were for excommunicating any Pársí who kept intercourse with any of the offenders then expelled from among them, but the latter would, and did, themselves eat and drink with those *outcasts*, even in Bombay, although the rules prohibited all from doing so; in short, one after another, each and every one of the rules and regulations passed by the late Pancháyat for the better government of the Pársís, have either directly or indirectly been suffered to be violated and trampled upon by these newly-made leaders; but the last, though not the least, cause of the division between the said old and newly-made leaders, was the encouragement given on the part of the latter to the unhappy re-establishment of the custom of bigamy among the Pársís, and which the old members strove hard to check and annihilate; and for which offence a number of their countrymen, from time to time, were excommunicated." Such were the objections urged ten years ago by a member of the community.

A Pancháyat still exists, but rather in character as a committee for the distribution of funds collected for charitable purposes,—the humiliating admission of "limited authority" in the memorial to Lord Auckland, of the 21st November 1838,—than the "efficient authority to control the vicious and encourage the virtuous." To the letter of the British Law do the Pársís now turn in every instance where justice is sought, and freedom from ancient and unseemly fetters is thus shown; to the spirit of the British character they should now direct the minds and energies of their offspring—thence they themselves will derive more durable happiness, present a noble rivalry as a race to surrounding natives in properly applied emulation, and bequeath that inheritance for which generations to come will honour them. That character does not consist so much in enterprise, or enthusiasm, or the honest pride of self-created wealth, or the veneration of ancestry, to be found as fairly developed in Pársís as in Englishmen; but it is in those principles which will permit them patiently to endure misfortune —whether poverty, undeserved calumny, or other calamity—and to tread the great battle-field of life, even in the face of disasters, with the discipline of the soldier, and the well-sustained fortitude of the hero.

SECTION V.

Aptitude for Business and enterprising Spirit.—Partiality to Europeans.—Visiters to Europe.—Bankers to Native Chieftains, and of those engaged in a political Capacity.

In noticing the disposition of the Pársís, the writer has urged their gaiety of manner, their warmth of heart, their sociality of spirit among themselves, and a leaning to benevolence generally. In the business concerns of life, again, Pársís are apt, shrewd, industrious and persevering; keenly alive to their pecuniary interests, and prompt in availing themselves of an advantage, whatever the hazard or detriment to the party bargaining. To their unwarlike character must be attributed that pursuit of traffic which had engrossed their attention for centuries since their landing in Hindusthan; and, as has already been observed, the bent of the mind is still "purely commercial."

It is only of late years that they have betaken themselves to employment under Government, and other avocations. Thirty years ago there were but two Pársís employed as English copyists in a Government office, and some half-a-dozen in counting-houses: not only public offices, but banks, merchants' and attornies' offices, are now literally crowded with them. The tendency is wholly European, and this tendency both time and circumstance are likely to improve. While with that class who are not required to earn their livelihood from their independent means, not only do they profess a delight in English literature, but they subscribe to and read the newspapers of the day, and are members of literary societies. Another age will offer no singular statistics if this spirit of improvement should happen to continue: another generation will be either infidel, or adopt a faith more consonant to reason, and more worthy of Him who is adored.

Pársís were the first people in India

who made fermented liquors. The *sack* which killed the celebrated pedestrian, Tom Coryate, at Swálí, at the mouth of the river Taptí, is no other than the *máurá*, and the *beurá** is another variety of it. Arrack has also been distilled by the Pársís for centuries; this arrack was the ordinary liquor of Europeans in India to the close of the last century. To this day, a Pársí holds the contract from the Government of Bombay for the supply of arrack, and another the contract of the tobacco farm.

Other speculations have attracted attention. A Pársí contractor constructed, at the expense of Lady Jemshedjí Jíjíbhái, the Causeway between Mahim and Bandura; and the same party, it has been stated, holds the contract for completing the line of railway from Persíck Point to Kálían. Pársís, some twenty years ago, owned almost the whole of the splendid country

* The *beurá*, it ought to be remarked, is extracted from the wet fruit of the Date Palm (*Phœnix dactylifera*), imported from the Persian Gulf.

maritime fleet that used then to trade between Bombay and China; and not very long ago, some three or four Pársí families owned a very large proportion of the landed property in the Island of Bombay. The moment that the Local Government threw open to the native public large plots of land in the island of Salset upon tenures worth the possessing, the Pársís were the principal applicants. Carrying out the same earnest, enterprising spirit, Shet Frámjí Káuvasjí introduced the culture of the sugar-cane, mulberries, silk, and a variety of other exotics to the soil and to its natives. Others of the Pársí landed gentry of Salset constructed wells and roads, and, where desirable, introduced salt-pans. The benevolent measures of Sir Jemshedjí Jíjíbhái are world-wide. Dr Buist, in furnishing, in the "Annals of India for 1848," a statement in detail of the munificent acts of the Pársí knight, which in twenty-six years cost him "more than a quarter of a million sterling," makes the following very pertinent observation:—"History contains no example of a merchant, yet in the enjoyment of a green old age, still deeply engaged in business, who has neither heritage nor legacy left him, and whose fortune has arisen from the earnings of his own enduring enterprise and ability, with all his faculties in the most perfect integrity, and with a numerous flourishing and affectionate family around him, conferring sums so enormous as those enumerated, for purposes of philanthropy."* The Láují family were brought

* The following stanzas, from the pen of the writer of this brochure, appeared in the "*Gentleman's Gazette*," a Bombay newspaper, on the 22d January 1849. They accompanied an Anglo-autograph signature of Sir Jemshedjí Jíjíbhái, the Pársí Knight of Bombay, forwarded to a lady in England who was forming a collection of such souvenirs:—

What if an Eastern name you trace
  Upon the tablet that I send?
That name you must but justly place
  If with the good you would it blend.

Here 'mid the thousands of a race
  "The human" 'tis unaptly styled;
How little of it *human*—grace
  The man, the woman, or the child!

to Bombay from Surat in 1756, in consequence of their skill as master shipwrights;

Cunning and wealth attract it young—
With growing years this Hindu clay
O'er dark corruption well hath flung
The strength of youth, its manhood's day!

Among them rise a stranger band,
Expatriated from their home;
Yet o'er this sterile, sunny land
Their enterprise and fame are known!

Within this throng a name is shown
Familiar o'er the Indian seas—
Commerce and charity have borne
It far with each benignant breeze!

That name is too a household name
Within the compass of our Isle;
And well the Gabar's deeds may shame
Full many a generous wile—

Of Christian (with his glorious creed),
That cymbals forth his charity;
And if the hand be stretched in need,
The world should know it readily.

Go! view yon pile,* which lowly rears
Its graceful, elongated frame—
There, in that pile, the suff'rer shares
Comfort and care he ne'er could name!

* The Sir Jemshedjí Jíjíbhái Hospital will remain a monument of benevolence and sincere human sympathy, only fairly appreciated when its princely founder will have gone from his generation.

and members of the family continue to this day in the East India Company's Dock-yard in the like capacity,—drawing the most lucrative salaries.

Free at his feet assistance flow—
To probe the wound, or heal the sore,
Arrest the fever's raging glow,
And kill the danger to its core.

Thence turn thy gaze, and dwell a while
Upon the multitudes that cling
Restless and busy—yet who smile
Around the wells whose gen'rous spring

Supplies the waters which they need;
But in these sultry climes alone
We careful prize, as guarded heed
The crystal stream 'gainst drought well known.

"These wells you see," the drawers say,
"Were form'd by him who knows the poor;
If these sustain in famine's day,
Never to them is closed his door!"

And those exploits sublimely great—
Philanthropy enshrines right well;
Of which we read or proudly prate,
At his behest instinctive swell!

The leper's home—the beggar's hall—
The kindly word in sorrow's strife—
The ready purse, assuaging all
The agony and curse of life.

The Pársís and English have maintained a steady intercourse since the settlement of the latter at Surat; indeed, Pársís have

Oh! such a name is worthy place
In higher record than the page
Which marks the ev'ry written trace
Of statesman, soldier, and of sage!

The Rothschild of his exil'd race—
The Gresham of our Eastern isle—
The Wilberforce in deeds of grace!
Vainly doth fancy thus beguile?

Few are the good beneath the sun
We rightly prize when here with us;
But like yon orb, the race when done,
We know the worth then lost to us.

How cold had been our very praise—
How oft unjust the wrongful thought—
Employ'd *our* prism to tell *his* rays,
When diff'rent spheres had own'd our lot!

Ah! in those realms his faith doth own
Beyond the nether ken of earth!
If virtues rare have brighter shone
Among their own high kindred birth—

There, nigh Divinity—the bless'd—
A glorious as a longer reign:
By equal spirits well caress'd,
I know how justly he'll sustain!

9th November 1848.

ever shown a partiality for Europeans. A good many families may still be seen in the now ruined port of Damán, appertaining to the Crown of Portugal. Numbers of Pársís speak the garbled Portuguese, in use in India, with ease and fluency; particularly those who have been any time resident either at Macao in China, or in Damán. Some are acquainted even with French: the late Bhíkájí Ratanjí, a Pársí merchant, resident for many years at the Mauritius, was almost French in character, and wholly so in habits and manner of living. Louis Philippe, King of the French, presented the late Shet Jehángír Nasarwánjí Wádíyá with a gold medal, for the civilities paid his subjects upon visiting Western India. The late Shet Jíjíbhái Dádábhái also received some flattering mark of the approbation of the French Government. Shet Mánackjí Karshedjí met with a most distinguished reception from the French monarch, on a visit paid to the Court of the Tuilleries. While at Paris, Mánackjí was made a Freemason by the French fraternity; since then, others of his community have been initiated by the craft, in a lodge opened for the express purpose of admitting the natives of India.

When the Puritan chaplain of the English factory at Surat—Mr Henry Lord—published his work on the strange sects of the Pársís and Vániás, public attention was certainly engrossed by a subject which led to important disquisitions for nearly two centuries afterwards. The writer cannot trace, however, the visit of a Pársí to Europe before the close of the last century; and this is only casually noticed in an edition of Edmund Burke's Life and Writings. Maníar, a Pársí, accompanied by Haníman, a Hindu, appear to have then visited England as the agents of Bájí Ráu the Peshwá. They lived during the year 1781 at Beaconsfield, the residence of the illustrious English statesman: they conformed to their Indian mode of living, and especially to Indian diet. Both Pársí and

Híndu appear to have suffered severely during the winter. They returned to India in the course of the following year. The Peshwá's letter to Mr Burke has never been traced, but the statesman's communication in reply favourably names both his Indian acquaintances. To both he applies the expression *caste.* This Maníar, the Pársí, belonged to the Mancharjí Shet family, of Surat, who possess a portrait of him taken in oil-colours. The present members of the family merely remember his voyage to Europe; his papers with reference to this important voyage were destroyed by the great fire, which consumed their own house, along with numbers of others, some forty years ago. Just half a century afterwards from the time of Maníar's visit to London, a number of spirited young Pársís, of the most respectable families of their community, proceeded to London, bent upon information. Of these young men, Shet Mánakjí Karshedjí seems to have been best known to the European public, from the notice taken of him by members of the *haut noblesse* of Britain.* Shet Ardeshír Karshedjí, of the Láují family, devoted his stay in England to the study of mechanical engineering, and his companions to the recent improvements in ship-building. The members of the Court of Directors of the East India Company paid these gentlemen every personal attention, and promoted the purposes of their visit.

Rare instances offer among the Pársís as financiers to crowned heads, or holding diplomatic position. The late Shet Bohmanjí Mancherjí Bháunagrí acquired a fortune from humble beginnings in the territory of the Thákur of Bháunagar; his son obtained a pálkí—a mark of honour among native chieftains—from the Nawáb of Suchín, and was highly esteemed by both Mr Williams and Mr Sutherland, who successively held the high post of Resident at Baroda. The failure of the great banking-

* Appendix C.

house of Víkájí Meherjí at Bombay has been attributed to an unsettled liability of more than £400,000 sterling, claimed of His Highness the Nizam's Government. The opulent firm of Sir Jemshedjí Jíjíbhái has been for years, it is stated, the banking-establishment of several Indian potentates. The family of the daring native magistrate under the Bombay Government—Ardeshír Danjísháh Khán Báhádur—were noticed by the Mogul Emperors of Delhí, through the talent shown by an ancestor in watch-repairing, which led to the management of Jághírs. A descendant of this artisan was the agent of the Government of Bombay in procuring the last *phirmán*, or imperial authority, which they solicited or ever required. Another member of the same family was killed in the performance of a delicate but trying duty intrusted to him by our political chief at Surat. Mánakjí Meherwánjí Wakharíyá was agent for the Bombay Government at Surat for some time. Shet Karshedjí Mánakjí was the great Commissariat contractor to the Bombay forces towards the close of the last century, when the British were battling with political annoyances with empty coffers.

The brilliant, yet unfortunate, career of the most distinguished of their community who undertook the task of Government, deserves more than a hasty notice. During the period (extending from the year 1801 to 1809) of Colonel Close's political embassy at Puná, at the Court of the Peshwá,—"he was," according to Grant Duff, the historian of the Maharátas, "in the habit of receiving native visiters through an agent, a Pársí, named *Khasrují*, familiarly styled the *Mudí*: a person of comprehensive judgment, and of great address, who soon obtained considerable influence over his master. Sadáshíu Bháu Mánkesír, or Mánkesvar, (the accredited authority of the Government of Puná, in correspondence with the British Ambassador,) and the Mudí soon formed a compact; and having united with them Biyájí Náik, a Hajrá, or personal servant of the Peshwá, by whom Biyájí was much trusted as a spy, they contrived to persuade Bájiráu (the Peshwá) that by gaining Khasrují to his interests, he might command the services of the British Presidency: a proposal well suited to the mind of Bajírau, by whom no means were spared to attain an end so desirable. The triumvirate, in all probability, participated in the spoils; and all intercourse, public as well as private, went on so agreeably by the agency of those persons, that there was no cause of dissatisfaction. Any subject likely to occasion unpleasant discussion was either postponed, or so arranged, that before being brought forward on either side, it was smooth of its asperities: so that little difficulty remained in the adjustment. The services of Colonel Close during this year (1810) were called for, on a very important occasion, to Hidarábád, and he never returned to his situation at Puná. Mr Henry Russell succeeded to the temporary charge of that residency, until the return of

Mr Elphinstone from a mission to Kabul, and the same harmony continued to prevail. Khasrují, though a servant of the British Presidency, had been permitted to accept the high office of Sarsubedár (Deputy Lord-lieutenant of the Karnátík) under the Peshwá's Government, and he appointed as his deputy, a Brahmin named Bapu Sané. Mr Elphinstone's personal interference in all the affairs of his bureau, with the additional circumstance of a misunderstanding between Mankesír and Khasrují, led the latter to avail himself of such influence as he possessed to bias the mind of the Peshwá against our political resident, whom he alleged entertained the same views as General Wellesley (the late Duke of Wellington), against whom Bájí Ráu had an unwarrantable dislike. Though many endeavours were made, by resuscitating old and mixed inquiries, towards Khasrují being reinstated in his former position at the residency, the Peshwá "had soon reason to acknowledge the impartiality of the resident, on the subject from which his chief prejudice against him had arisen." From a love of political intrigue, which argued that those who acted for him might as often oppose him, he nominated Khasrují to the office already named. The Pársí's antagonist in the good will of the Peshwá took occasion not long after to acquaint his chief with certain malpractices of Khasrují in his government; but as he was a servant of the British, sundry charges were presented against him to the political resident by three of the creatures of the Peshwá and Mankesír. So soon, however, as his recall was effected, the Peshwá personally interfered to prevent further investigation, and the matter was burked with his personal presence in the vicinity of Puná. Mr Elphinstone subsequently urged the incompatibility of Khasrují being the governor of a Maharáta province, and his confidential employment with his mission; and required that a preference should be given for his future engagements;—he quitted the Peshwá's service for the British. But the continued ill-deportment of Khasrují Mudí, "which from the first had not escaped the resident's observation, became such as to render it necessary to remove him from Puná: in order to prevent, as far as possible, the bad effects of the dangerous opinions which he inculcated. His past services entitled him to all due consideration from the British Government; and it would have been both difficult and ill-judged to have proved the circumstances by which he had forfeited his claim to its reward. A liberal provision was, therefore, made for him in his native province, Gujarát; but, about the eve of his intended departure (1814) he died by poison. Whether it was administered by others, or taken wilfully or accidentally by himself, could never be discovered, although the case underwent a long and strict investigation. If he knew more secrets, with respect to foreign intrigues, than Bájí Ráu and Trímbakjí Dánglía (the Peshwá's premier) thought fit to trust to any third person beyond their own power, his death may be imputed to their machinations; but it was the general opinion of the people at Puná, that he had poisoned himself through a fear of the loss of reputation, when, by removal from power and office, his corrupt practices might become public. It is, however, remarkable, that in succession to this general report, the Peshwá, who had before quashed the proceedings against him, now became his accuser; and Bápu Sáuní, the deputy of the deceased, was called upon by Bájí Ráu to account for the defalcation, bribery, and corruption of his master. During the proceedings, Bápu Sáuní died suddenly—of fright, it was said, at what he might expect if proved delinquency threw him into the power of Trímbakjí Dánglía."

Much may be added regarding the eccentricities of particular families, but that tenderness to the feelings of their surviving relatives and friends forbids it. The following is so well known, that the writer does not hesitate in giving it:—The celebrated

Entí (signifying "the proud") family of Surat, had bequeathed to them a quarter of a million sterling, acquired in commercial speculations by their father. The family disagreed among themselves as to its apportionment, and the matter was referred to the Zilla Court; the money, of the old Surat currency, in the meanwhile being very carefully stored. After twenty years' litigation, the treasure-vaults were opened; and, upon payment of legal charges, and allowing for depreciation in value of the old coin, something like *seven* lakhs of rupees were divided among the surviving members.

Mention might also have been made of the different families now holding position among the community, only that the writer did not undertake to render the present publication a reference for pedigrees. But one family among the Pársís, by their own report, can trace anything like an ancestry,—that of the Dádí Shet,—and even they not beyond five generations.

PROPER NAMES

OF

THE PÁRSÍS OF BOMBAY.

Men.

Terminations in *sháh*.—Behrám, Bohman, Dhín, Dhanjí, Dárá, Manchar, Pheros, Sohoráb,—as Behram*sháh*, &c.

Terminations in *bháï*.—Dádá, Dhosá, Dhanjí, Hírjí, Jíjí, Náná.

Irregular Terminations.—Ardeshír, Jehangír, Káikhasru.

Terminations in *jí*.—Auder, Aspandhíyár, Bápu, Barjor, Behrám, Bezan, Bhíká, Bohman, Doráb, Dhan, Edal, Frám, Fromaz, Fardun, Gusthád, Hír, Hormasd, Jemshed, Jámas, Jívá, Jívan, Káuvas, Karshed, Kháikobád, Kuvar, Lím, Mának, Manchá, Meher, Meherwán, Nasarván or Nashírván, Náuroz, Pestan, Pálan, Ratan, Rustam, Shápur, Sohoráb, Támul, Venka, Víká.

WOMEN.

Terminations in *bái* in India, and *bhánu* in Persia.—(The significations of most of the names are given.)—Suná (*Gold*), Rupá (*Silver*), Mothí (*Pearl*), Hírá (*Diamond*), Phíroz (*Turquoise*), Mítí (*Sweet*), Gul (*Rose*), Málik (*Ruby*), Shírín (*Delightful*), Jar (*Gold-Thread*), Ratan (*Emerald*), Aván (*Air*), Kuvar (*Royal*), Dhan (*Wealth*), Chándan (*Moonlight*), Khursad (*Sun*), Bhíkái, Dhanbyí, Navaz, Vílar, and Sakar-Vahu (*Sugar-like*); Dhín and Meher (names of two of their angelic host).

APPENDIX.

A.

GUJARATI PUBLICATIONS.

The Bombay *Samáchár* (News), Sunday and Thursday.

The *Jám-i-Jámshíd* (Goblet of Jámshíd), Wednesday and Saturday.

The *Chábuk* (Whip or Lash), and Bombay *Harkáru* (Courier), Monday and Friday.

The *Samáchár Darpan* (News), daily.

The *Rásht-i-Goftr* (Truth-teller), Sunday.

The *Chítr-Dnyán Darpan* (Illustrated Knowledge), Tuesday and Friday.

The *Parsee Reformer*, Wednesday and Saturday.

B.

To the Honourable the GOVERNOR GENERAL, and LEGISLATIVE COUNCIL of INDIA, CALCUTTA.

The humble Petition of the undersigned principal Parsees, Inhabitants of Bombay, and Subjects of His Britannic Majesty,

Most respectfully showeth,—That the Parsees, from the time of the arrival of their ancestors in India, have been a distinct race; and although they may have adopted in some degree the dress and usages of the Natives of India, with whom they have intermingled, they have, as far as circumstances would permit, observed the forms of worship which were preserved by their ancestors, and such customs and regulations as have come down by tradition to the living generation. They are at the present time as distinct from Hindoos, Mahomedans, and Christians, as the Parsees who first found their way to India.

2. Your petitioners further have to state, that not having had any regular code of law which had prevailed in ancient times for their guidance respecting the succession to property after the death of persons of their religion, the Parsees

have generally divided the property, immovable and movable, of a deceased person, who has died without making a Will, according to certain usages, which have prevailed amongst the most wealthy and respectable families, and in some instances corresponding with the mode of distribution or division which has obtained amongst the Hindoos in this part of India.

3. These usages have so long been submitted to, and have been followed in so many instances, from generation to generation, that they have by many persons been considered to have the force of law.

4. It has also been the custom of the Parsees for many years past to make Wills in the English and in the Guzratty languages, and when the Wills have been made by a person of sound mind, and free from fraud, their validity has always been admitted, although not formally prepared or witnessed, according to the rules said to exist in England when the Wills of landed proprietors are executed.

5. Such Wills, from the time of the establishment of the Mayor's Court at Bombay, have been proved, and no instance is remembered by your petitioners in which the Will of a Parsee, dividing landed property, has been set aside, because it was not executed in the presence of three witnesses.

6. Until a very recent period, no questions have been raised respecting the rights of Parsees

to divide their landed property by Wills such as have been described, or to divide houses, oarts, lands, and pieces of ground, between the widows and children of Parsees who have not left Wills according to the usages before alluded to; and no distinction has existed from the nature of immovable and movable property; for, as with Hindoos and Mahomedans, both kinds have been valued and disposed of alike.

7. This was the state of things, your petitioners humbly represent, when the Recorder's Court was established; and when, for the first time, it was declared at Bombay, that in all actions and suits against the inhabitants of Bombay, their inheritance and succession to lands, rents, and goods, and all contracts and dealings between party and party, should be determined, in the case of Mahomedans, by the laws and usages of Mahomedans; and in the case of Gentoos, by the laws and usages of Gentoos; and when only one of the parties shall be a Mahomedan, or Gentoo, by the laws and usages of the defendant.

8. The Parsees were at that period as distinct from all classes, who were then governed by English law, as either Mahomedans or Gentoos; but they appear to have been left unnoticed by the legislature, no doubt because the charter of the Court at Bombay was made like the charter of the Courts at Madras and Calcutta, where few Parsees resided.

9. The inconvenience, however, was not felt while Parsees agreed among themselves, and kept themselves, and their family disputes and differences, from being taken into the Recorder's and Supreme Court; but persons who are interested in promoting litigation have of late prevailed on Parsees to institute suits and actions in the Supreme Court, and to contend that as Parsees are neither Hindoos nor Mahomedans, the inheritance and succession to lands, rents, and goods, should be determined according to English law; that land in Bombay is freehold property, and that the eldest son, as heir-at-law, is entitled to inherit houses and land to the exclusion of his brothers; and that all Wills not executed according to English law are null and void.

10. If the Supreme Court should determine in favour of the claims last enumerated, the greatest ruin and mischief would be occasioned; the present title to two-thirds of the land on the Island of Bombay would be disturbed; Parsees who now hold possession of valuable property, either in virtue of arrangements with their brothers and other relations, or by descents from them, and persons who have purchased from younger sons of Parsees, may all be involved in litigation, and ruinous consequences must ensue.

11. Your petitioners therefore most respectfully solicit that you will be pleased, in conjunction with your Legislative Council, to pass a

regulation, conforming and making valid all that has been done respecting the partition in the sale and purchase of landed properties, of whatever nature, where no fraud has prevailed; and further declaring that all persons lawfully claiming under them, who have been in the undisturbed possession of lands, houses, oarts, or other immovable property within the Island of Bombay during the period of twenty-five years now last past, in virtue of any Will, or of any partition, or division, or other family arrangement, or of any arbitration or award acquiesced in or carried into effect, or of any agreement lawfully entered into, shall be guaranteed in the possession of such property, and not be liable to be dispossessed thereof by any action, suit, or other proceedings.

12. That this is the object of your petitioners: but they submit to the wisdom of the Legislative Council as to the best mode of preventing litigation, which may seek to disturb just and honest transactions which have been entered into by Parsees, and by other persons who have purchased property from them, under the belief that such transactions were lawful, and according to the usages which had long prevailed among Parsees at Bombay.

13. That if this application cannot be complied with on the representation of your petitioners, they entreat the Legislative Council that they will, with the least practicable delay,

cause inquiry to be made at Bombay respecting the usages and customs that have hitherto prevailed among Parsees at Bombay, in respect of the making of Wills, and the partition of property; to the end that some legislative provisions may be made to conform all that has been done in virtue of such Wills, and in conformity with such usages and customs, and without fraud; and to protect those who may now be in the quiet possession of immovable property from future litigation.

14. Should your Honourable Government, in its wisdom, deem it expedient to consult the Honourable the Judges of His Majesty's Supreme Court of Bombay on this most important subject, we feel convinced their Lordships will bestow every consideration upon it, and suggest what they may deem necessary and expedient for the fulfilment of the urgent request we have thus most respectfully submitted to your consideration.

And your petitioners, as in duty bound, will ever pray.

NOWROJEE JAMSETJEE,
And others.

Bombay, 20th November 1835.

To the Right Honourable Sir ROBERT GRANT, G. C. H., Governor and President in Council, &c. &c. &c.

RIGHT HON. SIR,—We have the honour to enclose herewith a Petition addressed by the body of our nation to the Legislative Council of India; which we have most respectfully to request your excellency will be pleased to forward, with such recommendation as in your wisdom it may merit.

We have the honour to be,
Right Honourable Sir,
Your most obedient Servants,
NOWROJEE JAMSETJEE,
Bombay, 23*d March* 1836. And others.

No. 348 of 1837.

Bombay Castle, 28*th February* 1837.

JUDICIAL DEPARTMENT.

GENTLEMEN,—With reference to my letter, dated the 23d of August last, No. 1461, I am directed to transmit, for your information, the accompanying copy of a letter from the Secretary to the Government of India, dated the 30th ult., with enclosures; and to inform you, that the Right Honourable the Governor in Council will be happy to learn your sentiments regarding the proposed enactment, and to take into consideration any objections which the Parsee community generally may have to urge against its provisions.

I have the honour to be, Gentlemen,
Your most obedient Servant,
J. P. WILLOUGHBY,
Secretary to Government.

To NOWROJEE JAMSETJEE, Esq., and others,
Parsee Inhabitants of Bombay.

No. 8.

To E. H. Townsend, Esq.,

Acting Secretary to the Government of Bombay.

Legislative.

Sir,—With reference to your letter, No. 999, dated the 6th June last, with its enclosures, I am directed to forward to you, for submission to the Right Honourable the Governor in Council, the accompanying copy of a Resolution, and draft of proposed Act, having for its object to quiet the possession of estates already acquired by Parsees in the way of succession, whether according to the English Law of Inheritance, which might hitherto have been judicially applied to the case of such estates, or in pursuance of usages or family partitions acted on or acquiesced in by the parties whose interests were concerned; and to fix the law by which the succession to the estates of Parsees, either by inheritance or testamentary disposition, is to be regulated in future.

2. The draft will, of course, be published in the Official Gazette of the Presidency of Bombay; and I am desired to request, that any representation which may be offered on the subject may be submitted for the consideration of His Lordship in Council, accompanied by the sentiments of

the Right Honourable the Governor in Council, with reference to such representation.

I have the honour to be, &c.,

(Signed) W. H. MACNAGHTEN,
Secretary to the Government of India.

Fort William, 30th January 1837.

(Copy.)

FORT WILLIAM, LEGISLATIVE DEPARTMENT.

The 30th January 1837.

RESOLUTION.—It has been brought to the notice of the Governor General in Council, that landed property of great value, within the jurisdiction of the King's Courts, is now held by Parsees, to whom it has descended in conformity with Parsee usages, but not in conformity with the English Law of Inheritance.

2. The national usages of the Parsees are not, like the Hindoo and Mahomedan rules of inheritance, marriage, and succession, recognised by law; nevertheless, it appears to His Lordship in Council, that Parsees, who are in possession of land which they have inherited according to their national usages, and with the acquiescence of all interested parties, ought not to be disturbed in that possession. This appears to His Lordship in Council to be one of those cases in which the strict enforcement of the law would defeat the end for which laws are made, would render property insecure, and would shake the confi-

dence of the people in the institutions under which they live.

3. His Lordship in Council is disposed to enact, that real property within the jurisdiction of the King's Courts shall, as regards its transmission by the will of a Parsee testator, or on the death of a Parsee intestate, be taken to be, and to have always been, of the nature of chattels real.

4. This enactment will be restricted by two provisos: one of those provisos secures in their possession all who hold such property by what has hitherto been a strictly legal title; the other is intended to give legal validity to those family arrangements which Parsees have heretofore made according to their national customs, in cases in which no objection has been made to those arrangements.

5. In order that time may be given to Parsees who reside at a distance from Calcutta to express their wishes, His Lordship in Council has determined to leave a longer interval than ordinary between the first publication, and the final reconsideration of the Act which has been prepared on this subject.

The following draft of that Act is herewith published for general information:—

Act No. —— of 1837.

1. It is hereby enacted, that from the   day of   all immovable property, situate within the jurisdiction of any of the Courts established

by His Majesty's Charter, shall, as far as regards the transmission of such property on the death and intestacy of any Parsee having a beneficial interest in the same, or by the last Will of any such Parsee, be taken to be, and to have been, of the nature of chattels real, and not of freehold.

2. Provided always, that in any suit-at-law, or in equity, which shall be brought for the recovery of such immovable property as is aforesaid, no advantage shall be taken of any defect of title, arising out of the transmission of such property upon the death and intestacy of any Parsee having a beneficial interest in the same, or by the last Will of any such Parsee, if such transmission took place before the said day of ; and if such transmission were either according to the rules which regulate the transmission of freehold property, or else took place with the acquiescence of all persons to whom any interest in that property would, according to the rules which regulate the transmission of chattels real, have accrued upon the death of such Parsee.

Ordered, that the said draft be reconsidered at the first meeting of the Legislative Council of India after the 9th day of May next.

(Signed) W. H. MACNAGHTEN,
Secretary to the Government of India.

(True copy)

J. P. WILLOUGHBY,
Secretary to Government.

To J. P. WILLOUGHBY, Esq.,

Secretary to Government, &c. &c. Bombay.

SIR,—In reply to your letter, No. 348 of 1837, handing us a copy of a letter from the Secretary to the Government of India, with enclosures, we have to request that you will be pleased to convey our best thanks to the Right Honourable the Governor in Council, for the important information thus afforded to us; and also to state that the proposed enactment entirely and most completely meets the views and wishes of the Parsee community; and that we have no objections whatever to urge against it. We trust we may also be permitted to request that the Right Honourable the Governor in Council will be pleased to convey to the Government of India the expressions of our warmest gratitude for the readiness with which it has met our views, in the framing and promulgation of an enactment, which will be of the most important service to the whole Parsee community of India.

We have the honour to be, Sir,
Your most obedient and very humble Servants,
NOWROJEE JAMSETJEE,
And others.

Bombay, 6th April 1837.

LEGISLATIVE DEPARTMENT.

Fort William, the 15th May 1837.

The following Act, passed by the Right Honourable the Governor General of India in Council, on the 15th May 1837, is hereby promulgated for general information :—

Act No. IX. of 1837.

I. It is hereby enacted, that from the 1st day of June 1837, all immovable property, situate within the jurisdiction of any of the Courts established by His Majesty's Charter, shall, as far as regards the transmission of such property on the death and intestacy of any Parsee having a beneficial interest in the same, or by last Will of any such Parsee, be taken to be, and to have been, of the nature of chattels real, and not of freehold.

II. Provided always, that in any suit-at-law, or in equity, which shall be brought for the recovery of such immovable property as is aforesaid, no advantage shall be taken of any defect of title arising out of the transmission of such property upon the death and intestacy of any Parsee having a beneficial interest in the same, or by the last Will of any such Parsee, if such transmission took place before the said 1st day of June 1837; and if such transmission were, either according to the rules which regulate the transmission of freehold property, or else took place with the acquiescence of all persons to whom any interest in that property would, according to the rules which regulate the transmission of chattels real, have accrued upon the death of such Parsee.

W. H. MACNAGHTEN,
Secretary to Government of India.

From the Honourable Sir John WITHER AWDRY, Knight, Puisne Judge of the Supreme Court of Bombay, to BOMANJEE HORMUSJEE, Esq.

Belair, 25*th April* 1837.

MY DEAR SIR,

I have much pleasure in returning to you the questions and answers relating to the usages of the Parsees: they seem to me to contain the groundwork of every practicable and civilized statute for the distribution of their property.

It is true that the law of England does not generally allow married women the possession of separate property without the intervention of trustees; but as their right to it with such intervention is fully recognised, there can be no objection in principle to its being allowed to those with whose manner it is accordant. It will, however, require attention to the framing a law, which will protect them in the enjoyment of it. It does not appear that it is intended that it should be in the power of a married woman to dispose of her inheritance, except by Will. If, however, so intended, it should be expressly provided for, and the means by which it could be ascertained whether a proposed conveyance of her property is her own free act, and not under any compulsion from her husband, must be considered. The modes provided in England for this purpose, in cases where the law empowers her to part with her inheritance, involve, as their most important ingredient, her examination, in the absence of her husband, by some trustworthy public officer, in order to ascertain whether she understands the nature of the act she is about to do, and does it by her own free will. The same observation, as to the necessity of considering how she is to be protected from the danger of undue influence in making her last Will, is even more important, because the difficulty of arriving at the truth is greater after her death. For the same reason, also, there is much greater danger of forgery. In England, a power to leave property by Will is often given to a woman by her marriage settlement, and the plan commonly adopted to authenticate such a Will is the provision that it shall be attested by disinterested witnesses. It will be observed that this matter requires the more attention here, as the Parsee women, though enjoying very high consideration, are not in general able to write, which English women of any substance always are; and, consequently, one great check upon forgery or deceit as to the nature and effect of a Will is wanting.

As the securing a wife's disposal of her property from the consent of her husband is justly considered by the Parsee community very important, I have thrown out these few observations to draw your attention to the means of enforcing it.

I quite concur in your wish that the Punchayet may be placed on a footing which will enable that body still to command the respect of your nation,—that it should be invested with some definite authority in ecclesiastical and matrimonial questions. As the subject is a very delicate one, I will only advert to one point, which is connected with the subject of inheritance. I hope that it will be empowered to decide in such mode as the Civil Courts can recognise, on the validity of all marriages between Parsees. An enactment, that on these points the usages of Parsees should have the force of law, would I think be desirable; but, on questions of property, I do not think such an enactment could have any other effect than that of letting in all that uncertainty which it is the object of passing a law on the subject of inheritance to prevent. The provision that illegitimate children should be entitled to maintenance I conceive to be just and wise; but I should recommend attention to be paid to the question—what summary mode of asserting and proving the right to it can be devised?—as it may otherwise have the effect of involving families in vexatious litigation.

On one very important point, I regret to think that my observations will not be satisfactory to you, though your anxiety on the subject is natural, and, perhaps, under your circumstances, praiseworthy. I do not think that the Legislature can or ought to give effect to your wishes, that a Parsee who changes his religion should forfeit his right to inheritance; because—

1*st*, Though doubtless such must always have been the wish of the Parsee community, no such usage can in Bombay ever have had any legal operation. From its nature, it evidently never can have prevailed by the consent of all persons interested, for the person chiefly interested must always have been averse to it. Nor can it have been enforced by Courts of Justice, for no Act of Parliament has ever enacted anything which would warrant their doing so. Being, then (in Bombay at least), a new enactment, and not an existing usage, it would be

2*d*, Completely at variance with that spirit of toleration to which provisions for the separate enjoyment by the Parsees of a system of property framed in accordance with their wishes are due, and which requires that a man's religion should not obstruct his enjoyment of the right of property.

3*d*, It is unnecessary; for the owner of the property may disinherit him by Will.

I will conclude, as I have begun, by expressing my conviction, that if the Parsees are really agreed on the proposed scheme of inheritance, the difficulty of framing a Statute to that effect (though greater than would be anticipated by persons unused to legislation) would be as little as can ever be expected in such cases, as the whole appears to be a very sensible and coherent system. I would, however, on questions 2, 3, wish to draw attention to the expression in 2—"her daughters and her grand-daughters"—ought it not rather to be, as in 3, the daughters and their issue; but, if not, in what proportions will they take? If, for instance, a woman dies, leaving a daughter and two grand-daughters, the daughters of a son, and other daughters of daughters, will each person take equally, or will the grand-daughters take no more than what would be their mother's share—and what will the daughters of a son take? This will lead to confusion, unless it is either very particularly laid down, or else the simple rule is adopted, that the heirs of a deceased child shall share amongst them in the usual proportion their parent's portion. With every wish that the proposed enactment may be conducive to the welfare of the Parsee people,

I remain, my dear Sir,

Yours very faithfully,

J. W. Awdry.

To the Honourable JAMES FARISH, Esq.,
Governor and President in Council, &c., Bombay.

HONOURABLE SIR,

We have the honour to enclose herewith a letter, which we have addressed to the Right Honourable the Governor General and the Legislative Council of India, which we beg most respectfully to request you will forward to that high authority: but, before handing it to the Government of India, with, we trust, the favourable recommendation of your Honourable Board, we would beg to solicit that you will be pleased to communicate with the Honourable the Judges of the Supreme Court, in order that we may benefit by the great experience and judgment of the present Chief Justice, the Honourable Sir Herbert Compton, who, in a pre-eminent degree, is qualified to offer an opinion upon the subject matter of our communication, and his able coadjutor, the Honourable Sir John Awdry.

2. We have no doubt that the Right Honourable the Governor General, and the Legislative Council of India, will be induced to concede the most considerate attention to the appeal we have made; and we congratulate ourselves upon Mr Borradaile having been appointed to a seat in the Law Commission, as that gentleman possesses an intimate acquaintance with all our peculiar customs and usages, and, from expe-

rience, can best speak to the necessity that exists for those customs and usages being recognised and confirmed by a legislative enactment.

We have the honour to be,
Honourable Sir,
Your most obedient and humble Servants,
FRAMJEE NUSSERWANJEE,
And others.

Bombay, 21*st November* 1838.

To the Right Honourable LORD AUCKLAND,
Governor General of India, &c. &c.

MAY IT PLEASE YOUR LORDSHIP,

We have the honour herewith, with great respect, to hand up for your Lordship's consideration a series of questions and answers, embracing the rights of inheritance that are acknowledged by the Parsee nation, and upon which it is the anxious desire of all who have the interests and welfare of our people at heart, that a Regulation should be framed by your Lordship, and the Legislative Council of India.

2. These questions were submitted by Harry Borradaile, Esq., the Registrar of the Adawlut Court of Surat, a gentleman intimately acquainted with all the peculiar rights and customs of the Parsee people. In framing the answers which are here subjoined, we beg to assure your Lordship that we have given the most patient

and reflective consideration to the subject; that we have consulted all the accessible testimony, both oral and written, and that we have discarded from our minds every feeling that might bias or pervert the true meaning and intention of our ancient and most revered laws. We trust we may also venture to submit to your Lordship that we consider the happiness, the welfare, the respectability, and the internal peace of our caste, to be intimately and inseparably associated with the passing of such a Regulation as we here presume to crave from the wisdom of your Lordship and the Legislative Council of India.

3. We deem it at once advisable to state, for the information of your Lordship, that objections have been made to some parts of our answers,—more especially to those in which the rights of inheritance have been conceded to the female branches of families; but these objections, we regret to say, have originated in interested motives, and it is for this reason that we have so carefully guarded, in our answers to question No. 1, against a husband exercising any control over property that his wife may have brought from her father's house. We know this is contrary to the law of England, but in our case it is absolutely necessary, for the prevention of domestic contention, and the thousand numberless evils that would arise to females were it otherwise. However desirable unanimity might be on such a

question, we could not consent to obtain it by sacrificing the rights of those who, from their weakness, more forcibly call upon our protection. Your Lordship, we feel confident, will judge between us with impartiality, and we fearlessly commit the interests of all concerned to your justice and benevolence.

4. If, as we hope, your Lordship and the Legislative Council of India may be graciously pleased to pass a Regulation in conformity with our desires, the next point to be considered is the enforcement of such Regulation. The Panchayet, we regret to inform your Lordship, is now almost powerless, either for good or evil; and unless that body is made respected by the Act of Government, the most serious consequences must ensue to the best interests of our caste. So long as the caste continued limited in number, and willing to obey the decisions of the Panchayet, the want of recognised authority in that body did not appear so forcibly as it now does to the feelings and understandings of those interested in the welfare and prosperity of the Parsee nation. Of late, however, a new spirit has sprung up, and each man claims a right of acting as he may think fit, and very often in defiance of the decisions of the Panchayet, and in wilful opposition both to the spirit and letter of our laws and usages. To be useful, and of avail, both the law, and those who administer it, must be respected—and re-

spect in ignorant minds seldom exists without some portion of fear. The lower orders of Parsees see that the Panchayet has no power to punish, and therefore do not respect its authority or its decisions, and as it has hitherto been our pride, and almost the wonder of surrounding people, that so large a body as the Parsees now comprise should be self-governed, we are led thus most urgently to pray that your Lordship will invest the Panchayet with an efficient authority to control the vicious and encourage the virtuous. Even with the limited authority that the Panchayet now possess, it is the source of much good. One instance will be sufficient to exemplify this to your Lordship, and that is, that the Parsee poor are entirely supported by the funds of which that body is the guardian and distributor. As bearing upon this grateful subject, we trust we may be permitted to bring to the notice of your Lordship an extract from the published report of the Bombay District Benevolent Society, which appeared in the *Bombay Courier* of the 27th August 1836,—a Society patronized by the Bombay Government, and some of the most influential of its officers. The passage we allude to is as follows:—"The public at large owe a debt of gratitude to the Parsees of Bombay; for not one beggar of that caste has ever applied to this Society for relief, nor is a Parsee pauper ever to be seen in our streets."

5. In the constitution of the Panchayet, in the selection of its members, and in the rules for its guidance, we are the first who would wish and pray for the most unceasing vigilance and control of the Local Government. We seek for no individual power or aggrandizement: the welfare, the happiness, the respectability of our caste, and the inviolability of our religion and peculiar customs, is all that we are desirous to promote. The strongest feeling entertained by a Parsee is that of veneration for his religion, and next to that may be ranked the extreme susceptibility that even the poorest and least instructed feel, as to any encroachment or interference with their customs and domestic manners. The enlightened Government of which your Lordship is the head, we full well know, will never sanction anything that could in any way hurt the feelings or prejudices of our caste; and our only anxiety is, by securing to ourselves a recognised authority for our self-governance, to make our people more respected, and more worthy of the continued favour and protection of the enlightened Government of British India.

6. In conclusion, we have also most respectfully to request that your Lordship and the Legislative Council of India will, by this proposed Regulation, recognise and confirm all usages, rights and customs, that have prevailed, and still prevail, among the Parsee people, which

will most materially tend to set at rest all doubts which may have arisen from the present imperfect and undefined state of our laws and regulations, and also best carry out the benevolent intentions of His Majesty's Ministers and the United Parliament of England, as set forth in the 53d Section of the New Charter Act.

We have the honour to subscribe ourselves,

My Lord,

Your Lordship's most obedient,

Most humble Servants,

NOWROJEE JAMSETJEE,

And others.

Bombay, 21*st November* 1838.

Answers to a series of Questions put by H. BORRADAILE, Esq., *relative to the Rights of Inheritance prevailing among the Parsees.*

Question 1*st.*—If a man dies without making a Will, to whom, and in what proportion, does his property descend?

Answer.—His son becomes his heir by right. If there is not a son, then his daughter and widow are his heirs, to each of whom a moiety of the property left belongs. The daughter's portion remains under the control of the mother until she becomes of full age, viz. eighteen years, and, after that, it is at her own disposal.

If there are neither sons nor daughters, then the widow is the true heir to all the property left. If the deceased leaves both a son, a daughter, and a widow, then the son becomes the heir, and it is his duty to collect all his father's property, and discharge all his just debts, within thirteen months of his decease; and whatever balance may then remain is to be divided as follows:—

1. To the deceased's sons, as many as there may be, belong twelve annas out of every sixteen annas left by the deceased, both of movable and immovable property, and which twelve annas are divided in equal proportions among all the sons: thus, if there are two sons, then to each appertain six annas; and if three sons, four annas each, and so on.
2. To the widow belongs a portion of two annas, which she may dispose of, with whatever other property she possesses, by her last Will and Testament, either during her husband's life, or after his death. If she dies without making a Will, then to her daughters, as many as there may be, revert twelve annas of all the property she may leave, in like manner as the father's property reverts to the sons. If those daughters die and leave children, then to those children belong their mother's portion of their grandmother's property, and as many daughters

as there may be among those children, to them belong twelve annas, and to the sons four annas.

3. To the daughters of the deceased belong the remaining two annas of his estate, which their mother shall receive and hold, until they become of the full age of eighteen years, when she will divide it in equal proportions. The claim of the daughters is against the mother, as she, in the first instance, shall receive their proportion of her deceased husband's estate, and only pay it to them when they become of the age of eighteen years. Upon the daughters' portions those daughters' husbands have no claims whatever; neither are their signatures required. In the event of both father and mother being dead, then the daughters shall receive their own and their mother's portion, altogether four annas, from their brothers; and on those daughters becoming of the age of eighteen years, all of them, and all the sons, shall receive and divide the same among themselves, in the manner before stated. In the event of there being neither daughters, nor daughters' issue, alive, then all the property of the deceased woman reverts to her sons.

Question 2d.—Is there any difference between the male and female rights of inheritance?—If a wife possesses, besides immovable property, other goods and effects, brought from her father's house, who is the heir thereof?

Answer.—The difference has already been pointed out, as the male heir's inheritance is twelve annas, and the female's only four annas. If a woman, besides immovable property, has brought from her father's house any goods or other property, or has collected the same in her husband's house during his life, the same shall be disposed of as directed by her last Will and Testament. But if she dies intestate, then her daughters and their issue are her heirs, to them belonging twelve annas, and to her sons four annas. If there are neither daughters, nor the issue of daughters, living, then the whole reverts to her sons, and their issue; and when there is no heir living, either immediate or remote, then, whatever the deceased woman may have brought from her father's house shall be returned to him, or to his heirs, either male or female.

Question 3d.—If a man dies, leaving a daughter, an adopted son, a widow, and other relatives, then to whom does the inheritance of his property belong?

Answer.—According to the deceased's last Will, so shall his property be divided; but if he dies intestate, then his daughter and widow become his joint heirs, each taking one-half of the property left. If the daughter dies, then to her issue the said half shall descend; and if the widow dies, then the whole estate belongs to the daughter of the deceased, and her issue. The adopted son has no right or claim whatever, except by Will, unless in cases where the adoption has been formally made in writing, with the consent of all the nearest of kin, (and all he can demand is a present, according to the circumstances and means of him who adopted him,) which shall be decided, (if any dispute rises,) by the Panchayet.

Question 4th.—If a man has a grandson, and he enters into a second marriage, but has no issue by his second marriage, then who is his heir—his widow, or his grandson?

Answer.—The grandson is his lawful heir; but to a wife of a second marriage, as of a first, appertain the two annas, as before stated.

Question 5th.—Is there any difference in the rights of inheritance between a layman's and an Andiaroo's wife?

Answer.—No, none whatever.

Question 6th.—If a wife becomes her husband's heir, can the relatives of her said husband take any objections to her expending the wealth bequeathed to her?

Answer.—No objections can be taken, unless where there are children under age, and then the relatives, if they see the woman squandering away the wealth, may interfere, and can bring objections, so as to save as much as possible of the property left.

Question 7th.—Does any difference exist between the rights of inheritance of a wife, by a first and second marriage, or the issue of a first and second marriage?

Answer.—No, none whatever. The rights of wives and children by first and second marriages are exactly the same.

Question 8th.—If a man has children by a woman, not of the Parsee nation, or even by a Parsee woman illegally, and if he afterwards marries a Parsee woman, and has children by her, or has adopted a son, and he dies without making a Will, then in what manner is property divided?

Answer.—He who has children by a woman of another nation, or by a Parsee woman illegally, to those children belongs that which he may give by his last Will; and in cases where such men may die intestate, then to such children no right of inheritance belongs. Food and clothes shall be given to them by the deceased's heirs during their life, according to the wealth the deceased father may have left.* If the true wife has issue, then that issue is the heir. But

* As it is apprehended that the very ascertaining the amount of property which is to regulate the provision for natural children will in many cases lead to expensive litigation, and perhaps the ruin of respectable families, it is suggested, as the best mode of obviating this evil, that the Panchayet

if she has no children, and has not appointed the adopted son heir to her property by Will, such adopted son has no further claim than before set forth, according to the circumstances and property of the parties. In the event of there being no children, nor the issue of children, then the property belongs to the nearest next of kin of the deceased.

Question 9*th.*—If a man dies and leaves a Will, appointing an heir, who from absence cannot perform the ceremonies due to the memory of the deceased, can any other person, who, being on the spot, performs those ceremonies, dispute the rights of him who has been appointed heir by the last Will and Testament of a deceased?

Answer.—No, they cannot. The heir appointed by the last Will must always be considered the true and lawful heir, whoever may perform the religious ceremonies.

Question 10*th.*—If a man during life discards his own son, and puts him out from his house, and ultimately dies intestate, then does that son by right take a portion of his father's property or not?

Answer.—No son can be debarred from sharing in his father's property, except where he is disinherited by such father's last Will; and, there-

(in cases of dispute) should be empowered to award the amount of maintenance to be given, and that their award should be final, and without appeal.

fore, as the question is put, the son is clearly entitled to share in the property left by his father.

Question 11*th.*—If a man has two or three sons, one of which sons, by his own industry, has earned money, can the other brothers claim a portion thereof,—and, if they cannot, can the father do so?

Answer.—If a son earns money in a different trade or calling, and away from his father's house, then such wealth belongs exclusively to himself. But if in his father's business, and in his father's house, although he may have laboured much more than others, such wealth must be considered as his father's, and therefore all the other brothers are entitled to share equally after the father's death. On the death of a father, leaving two or more sons, one only of whom may be of age, it is not lawful for him to carry on the trade of the father until his brothers become of the age of eighteen years, and enter into a deed of co-partnership with him.

Question 12*th.*—When a division of property is made among people of your nation, what customs or rules regulate such division,—and is there any difference in the division of movable and immovable property?

Answer.—When the inheritance comes to be divided, then all the movable and immovable property is considered as alike, and the division made according to what has been before set forth.

Question 13*th.*—If three or four brothers are living jointly, and one of those brothers dies, leaving a widow, but no children, does such widow become the heir of the deceased's portion of the joint estate?

Answer.—The widow becomes the heir of the deceased's portion. But when a son has been adopted, with the mutual consent of all the parties, viz. the deceased, his widow, and brothers, by a written instrument,* and that adopted son afterwards takes the name of the deceased, then to him, of the portion, shall devolve twelve annas and to the widow four annas. If, however, the said widow again marries, then that portion does not belong to her, but the whole sixteen annas revert to the adopted son and heir.

Question 14*th.*—If a man, having children by a woman of another nation, brings those children into his house during life, or they come in after his demise, have they any claim or right to share in the property left by their father?

Answer.—Whatever is left them by Will they may enjoy, but they have no right of inheritance whatever; maintenance is given them according to the property of the father.

* The instrument by which a son may be adopted may be as simple as possible in form, but it should be imperative that it be signed by the adopter, his wife, and brothers, or nearest next of kin, and witnessed by three disinterested persons; and contain a clause, leaving it at the option of the adopted to cancel the same during life.

Question 15*th.*—Can a man disinherit his son, —And in what way?

Answer.—By his last Will and Testament a man can disinherit his son, but in no other way.

Question 16*th.*—How far does the force of a last Will extend in denying the right of inheritance to the lawful heir? And is there any difference between movable and immovable property; and, in making a last Will, is a man's and woman's power equal?

Answer.—A last Will imperatively decides the question of inheritance. There is no difference between the rights to movable and immovable property; and the power of making a Will is equal, as regards a man and a woman. If, however, a man holds a jagheer given by way of indulgence, or in repayment of services performed by his family, and which jagheer by its condition is to descend from father to son in that family, no last Will, however made, can alienate such jagheer; the heirs and representatives of the family being fully entitled to all it may produce.

Question 17*th.*—If a man, by his last Will, not only cuts off his children, but also all his other relatives, and leaves all his property to some other person, is such Will considered valid, and is the inheritance of his children entirely annulled?

Answer.—Yes, provided that it can be proved that he was of sound mind when he made his

Will. But there are cases in which such Wills would be disputed, and set aside; as, for instance, where a man has been living with a woman of another nation, and has not conformed to the customs of his own people, and is ultimately cajoled into making a Will, leaving all to such woman, or to people of another nation, and, without fault on their side, setting aside entirely his natural and lawful heirs; then such Will would be annulled, and the property revert to his proper heirs. The same rule also applies in the case of a woman. If a Parsee (man or woman) becomes converted to the Christian, Hindoo, or Mahomedan faith, he forfeits all right and title to participation of property, or other benefits that might have accrued to him had he remained true to his own faith; and he is no longer looked upon or recognised as a Parsee. This forfeiture of all rights on the part of parents does not apply to the children who may remain true to their faith, and to them shall descend the portions of their parents.

Question 18*th.*—When a man dies without any children, and leaves a Will, making his wife his heir, with a stipulation that she shall adopt a son, which she afterwards does, and settles a portion of the property on such adopted son by writing, has such adopted son any claim upon the whole property, and can such woman leave to any other person, by her last Will, such portion of the property as she retained for herself?

Answer.—The adopted son has no claim upon the man's property, except to the extent of that which has been given him: that part reserved by the woman for herself she may dispose of by Will as she pleases; and, if she dies without making a Will, then it reverts to her legal heirs and representatives, but not to the adopted son.

Question 19*th.*—At the time of marriage, besides the jewels and joys given to the girl by the father and mother-in-law, is it the custom for his own father and mother to make similar presents; and, if so, can the husband exercise a control over such property? After the wife's death, who inherits such personal property?

Answer.—Whatever presents of joys and jewels may be received from the father and mother-in-law, over such have the husband and wife a joint control and authority, and at her death they revert by right to her husband and his heirs. But such things as she may bring from her own father's or mother's house, consisting of joys or jewels, are her own sole property, over which the husband can exercise no control or authority whatever; and she can, by her last Will, distribute the same as she may think fit.* In the

* As women are very liable to be unduly influenced and controlled in the bequeathment of their own property, and as it is much desired to secure to them the full and free exercise of their right, it is suggested that every Will by a woman leaving property must be witnessed by three disinterested persons.

event of her dying intestate, and there being no children, then all such property as she may have brought from her father's or her grandfather's, or her nearest relation's house, reverts to such party. If she leave children, but no Will, then the daughters shall receive three-quarters, and the sons one-quarter of such property, as regards joys and jewels received from the husband's relatives; if the woman in life is desirous of making a Will for the bequeathment of such property, she may do so, with her husband's consent, but not otherwise.

Bombay, 18*th August* 1836.

C.

India Board, the 29th November 1841.

SIR,—I have been requested to introduce to you a Parsee gentleman, who will have the honour of presenting this letter. It has not been without hesitation that I address one with whom I have not the pleasure of personal acquaintance, and of whom I can have no knowledge but from his reputation and distinguished services.

I presume, however, and hope that you will consider the official situation in which I have the honour to stand to the Governor of Bombay sufficient excuse.

The bearer of this introduction, Manackjee Cursetjee, will not have been unknown to you by name, and is a member of the Literary Society in your Presidency.

He was noticed on his arrival in England by the President of the Board of Control, and by the other members of the late ministry. He has since been known to Sir Robert Peel and myself, through the medium of Lord Clare, who was acquainted with him during his residence in the East.

Sir Robert Peel has expressed a wish that I should not leave you in ignorance of the favourable impression which Manackjee Cursetjee has

K

produced on those to whom he has been presented in England, with respect to his general acquirements, as well as the information which he has afforded to those who have conversed with him on the state of India.

He has given me, what I consider, important materials on the subjects upon which I inquired.

It has given me much satisfaction to find that one of your predecessors has appointed a native of ability in the public service, and I doubt not that the Government at home will rejoice with me to find that opportunities are taken for promoting the natives of India, and thus raising them in their own estimation, when individuals among them are found qualified to have a similar distinction.

I have the honour to be,

Sir,

Your very obedient and faithful Servant,

FITZGERALD AND VESEY.

To Sir W. MACNAGHTEN, Bart.,

Governor of Bombay.

THE END.